AROUND THE WORLD IN 80 DAYS
ALMANAC

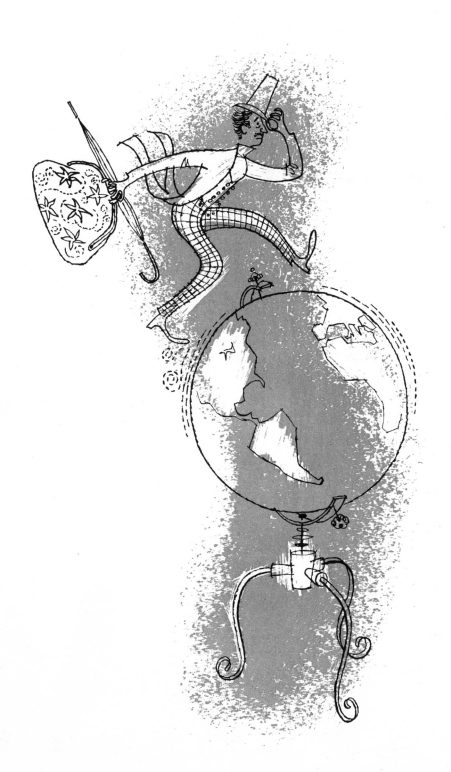

MICHAEL TODD'S
AROUND THE WORLD
IN 80 DAYS
ALMANAC

Edited by ART COHN

RANDOM HOUSE · NEW YORK

Aᴛᴛᴇʀ the opening of *Up in Central Park* in the Philadelphia tryout almost a dozen years ago, Sigmund Romberg, the composer, finds me in the lobby and, considering how well the show went, I am surprised by the look of anguish on his kisser. His beloved Danube was never bluer.

"My music!" he groans. "You can't hear a note! Mr. Todd, if you don't order the orchestra to play louder—*much* louder!—you must take my name off the show."

I promise to look into the matter and do the right thing.

A few minutes later, Dorothy Fields, the librettist, comes up glaring as if I had just foreclosed a mortgage on her.

"Why did I write lyrics, *dear* Michael?" she hissed. "All you can hear is the *music*."

It is an unhappy and illogical world, I am beginning to think, when Howard Bay, my scenic designer, grabs my arm.

"Eleven hundred, Mike," he groans. "Eleven hundred bucks for a pot-belly stove—and what happens? Actors stand in *front* of it the whole time!"

Yes, it is an amazing business.

I am walking out of the theater after the tryout of *South Pacific* in New Haven. I am shaking my head mournfully and saying, "Tsk, tsk," when Josh Logan collars me.

"Was it that bad, Mike?" he asks.

"I'm shaking my head and saying, 'tsk, tsk,'" I explain, "because after this, nobody should ever produce a show again, it's that wonderful."

Later, along about three in the morning, I get a yen for some delicatessen and I go to New

Foreword

York and who do I bump into but Winchell, who is also looking for delicatessen and other tidbits.

"Walter," I inform him while my pastrami and lox is being bageled (I hate pastrami and lox, but what can you do when a sandwich is named after you?), "I have just seen the greatest show ever staged. Rodgers and Hammerstein . . ."

"You sound like you have a piece of it," interrupts Winchell, who has moments of skepticism.

"I wish I was an usher in it," I say.

Two days later, Billie Pyser, my wardrobe woman for many years, comes to my office. There's a tradition that all wardrobe women are in love with their producers. It started in a Warner Brothers picture. But this is neither here nor there, right now Billie is agitated, as we disciples of a dear and departed Broadway bard say, more than somewhat.

"I've worked for only three producers," she says with a heavy sigh. "First, the great Florenz Ziegfeld, may he rest in peace. Then the wonderful Sam Harris, may he rest in peace. And now you, Mr. Todd."

"Get to the chorus, Billie," says I, "before I'm resting in peace too."

"I can't believe it," she says. "I just can't believe it."

"What?" I ask.

"I heard Walter Winchell's program last night. And do you know what?"

I dummy up. I'm not going on record that I didn't catch him. You never can tell who's doing undercover work for W. W.

"He said," says Billie, "that you called *South Pacific* the greatest show you had ever seen.

Say it isn't so, Mr. Todd."

"I'd like to help you out," I tell her. "But Winchell never misquotes anyone, not this time anyway."

"Oh, no!" Billie shudders. "You didn't . . . you couldn't!"

"*South Pacific* is everything I said it was," I insist. "Wait until you see it."

"I saw the dress parade," she says defiantly and ganders me with a kind of pity. "You like *that* show!" She holds up the thumb and forefinger of her right hand about half an inch apart, contemptuously. "The seams in the dresses are *this* thick."

Billie is serious. Everyone in every department of a show — as I suppose, in every organization — sees only his own work. To him, no matter how minute the detail, it is the most important. And do you know something? It is.

A producer has to see all the seams *and* everything else.

There are more seams in *Around the World in 80 Days* than in any other show in history. At least in my history.

It is the purpose of this Almanac to show you a few of them.

Thanks for dropping in. I hope you didn't mind the slight formality at the box office. Like many a notable demimondaine, I feel guilty about being compensated for doing the thing I enjoy most, and I would prefer to abolish the embarrassing practice. But this is a democracy and some of the Billie Pysers, despite their meticulous pride in their work, don't mind the Saturday night envelope, which now comes on Wednesdays.

Still you wonder, and as Bob Sherwood used to say, the theater is the dwelling place of wonder.

See It Now

by
EDWARD R. MURROW

(The prologue consists of scenes made at the turn of the century by George Melies, as well as shots of a guided missile at White Sands, N. M., and also shots taken so high above the earth that one can actually see the receding shape of the earth. The prologue, after being assembled, seemed unbelievable despite its authenticity, so Mr. Todd secured a commentator who would give credence to it. Hence, Edward R. Murrow.)

PROBABLY since man began to walk upright he has been interested in space and speed. He has sought to travel farther and faster than his forebears and he has succeeded. The stretching fingertips of science have moved him higher and faster.

Jules Verne, a writer bold in his predictions, conceived almost a hundred years ago what was then regarded as fantastic fiction but which has now become fact: the submarine, television, rockets. He wrote a book about going around the world in eighty days — he even predicted it would be done in eighty hours — and was, of course, laughed at. But with all his imagination, Verne did not shrivel the earth to the size it has now become.

The speed of transportation, communications and ideas has made this planet a whispering gallery which echoes both the threat and the promise created by the scientist. As time and distance contract, boundaries provide diminished defense against both hope and destruction.

Man has devised a method of destroying most of humanity or of lifting it to high plateaus of prosperity and progress never dreamed of by the boldest dreamer — a world without famine, without disease, a world of unlimited power and limitless hope.

Speed is good when wisdom leads the way. The end of this journey, whether to the high horizons of hope or to the depths of destruction, will be determined by the collective wisdom of the people who live on this shrinking planet.

Contents

This book was produced by Ray Freiman

Around Mike Todd in Eighty Moods

by ART COHN

AS OTHERS SEE HIM

"He is an Oxford man posing as a mug."—George Jean Nathan, a Cornell man.

"He definitely belongs on a runaway horse."—Joe E. Lewis, horse player.

"He has the soul of a pitchman and the ambition of a Napoleon."—John Chapman in *Colliers*.

"He's half-smart to everything"—*The New Yorker.*

"He is the greatest natural gambler I've ever known and the most spectacular of all the many colorful figures that have passed through the Broadway producing scene in the past thirty years or more. He is enormously good-natured, worldly wise in every way and one of a mob."—Damon Runyon.

"The dizzying history of Todd's promotion—carnival roustabout, trustee of a bricklaying academy, bankruptcy-sale impresario, building contractor, movie studio soundproofer, plunger on horses and cards, dramatist, director and, of course, all-around switch-hitting showman. In all of these roles—including, and even particularly, that of bankrupt—he has maintained such unshakable self-confidence that his career is worth study as a classic example of that quality."—Joel Sayre in *Life*.

"He may parlay himself into the poorhouse or Fort Knox; but in either case, he will sup on caviar and champagne."—Abel Green in *Variety*.

"Three characteristics set him apart as a unique man. First, he never runs out of ideas. Second, he is a peerless salesman. Last and most important, after he has lived an experience, good or bad, he can walk away from it, without looking over his shoulder."—Michael Todd, Jr.

"Although he has always lived high, wide and handsome and has been a spectacular gambler, he is a straight-shooter and his credit is practically unlimited."—Maurice Zolotow in *The Saturday Evening Post*.

"The most wonderful thing about him is he's so soft. Wherever you touch him, pure cashmere."—Betty Garrett, actress.

"He's happiest when the going is roughest. If he has a flop in Boston, he's in."—Dorothy Fields, playwright.

"He is almost certainly going to be a legend."—John K. Hutchens, *New York Times Magazine* (May, 1945).

AS HE SEES HIMSELF

"A producer is a guy who puts on shows he likes. A showman is a guy who puts on shows he thinks the public likes. I like to think I'm a showman. I'm not interested in social significance, symbolism or artistic triumphs that are financial losers. I worship artistic integrity, but in a public medium success is determined solely by public *acceptance*, and that is ascertained, unfortunately—or fortunately, according to the point of view—by the slight formality at the boxoffice.

"You can't teach showmanship—because there are no rules. If there were rules it would not be showmanship.

"I've been broke many a time but I can honestly say I've never been poor. Poverty is a state of mind. When you start thinking with your wallet, you're always wondering what you *can't* do instead of what you can do, and you're never going to get off your back.

"Don't get too analytical, you'll overdrive the green.

"There are no geniuses around. If there were, I'd be self-conscious.

"I admire honesty, because most people who are on the take always whisper and I prefer to shout. Nothing I can buy could give me as much pleasure as raising my voice: for what I like and against what I don't like.

"The life of a showman is a hard way to make an easy living."

AS I SEE HIM

A five-foot-nine, 152-pound bundle of energy and wonder: gifted, grandiose and resourceful, a bold man fighting middle-age as if he were going to beat it.

A compulsive talker and cigar smoker—unable to sit or stand still, he is a slave of action. It is signicant that his first film production exalts a man who races the clock around the globe.

He is primitive and original. Born Avrom Hirsch Goldbogen in Minneapolis, son of a Polish rabbi, he evolved his present name from Toad, his nickname, and his son's first name. A senior named after a junior!

As a boy in Minneapolis, Bloomington, Minnesota, and Chicago, he smelled all the flowers: newsboy, fruit peddler, cornetist, pitchman's shill, carnival come-on, soda jerk, at thirteen the youngest apprentice pharmacist in Illinois, shoe salesman, a high-pressure merchandising Wallingford, founder of a bricklaying college, and at seventeen, president of a construction company and married.

Before he was twenty, he had become an "expert" at soundproofing movie stages in Hollywood and was also in the lumber, paving and steamship businesses. He made a fortune fast and lost it faster. By 1933 he was a gag writer for Olsen and Johnson, and producer of a Flame and Moth Girl show at the Chicago Century of Progress Exposition. A dancer would flutter close to a huge candle until her gauzy wings and leotard caught fire, then she would scamper off stage apparently without clothes. "I burned up four girls before I got it," he recalls.

He conquered Broadway in 1939 with his first hit, *The Hot Mikado,* starring Bill (Bojangles) Robinson, backed with a soap bubble waterfall forty feet high and a volcano that erupted. Burns Mantle of the New York *News* hailed the show as "absolutely unrivaled so far as my playgoing experience is involved."

He had four shows at the New York World's Fair, then made Broadway history with a glorified burlesque at $4.40 tops, *Star and Garter,* which ran 609 performances; *Something for the Boys,* with Ethel Merman, 422 performances; *Mexican Hayride,* with Bobby Clark, 504 performances; *Up in Central Park,* 504 performances; and such other triumphs as *Hamlet,* with Maurice Evans, which received rave notices; *Catherine Was Great,* with Mae West, that ran 191 performances in New York and made a fortune on the road; and *The Naked Genius* with Joan Blondell, who, after the death of his wife in 1947, became the second Mrs. Todd, a union that lasted three years.

He had four smashes running simultaneously on Broadway. "I was a Boy Wonder," he recalls. "That was before I became a Boy Failure."

Hot tips and cold dice sent him, in 1947, into involuntary bankruptcy, with liabilities of $1,105,616.78. During the proceedings he maintained his usual privileged standard of living: a home in Westchester County in addition to a lavish penthouse apartment and offices that covered seven floors and accommodated a staff of twenty-one. "I owed a million and a half," he explains. "What was I supposed to do—cut down on my cigars?"

While he was in hock, he raised $375,000

and produced a roughhouse musical comedy, *As the Girls Go,* that ran 420 performances. Then he signed Phumiphon Aduldet, a jazz musician who was also King of Thailand, formerly Siam, to write two songs for a musical, *Peep Show,* which ran 278 performances. How good were the King's songs? "If Benny Davis had written them," confesses Todd. "I wouldn't have bought them."

In 1950, after he had paid back more than $850,000 of his debts, the court withdrew the bankruptcy petition—at his request. It figured. A true gambler doesn't welsh. Also, he had spent many years creating the name of Mike Todd: it was his passport, his most precious possession. And he didn't want the stigma hanging over Mike Junior. In his words: "I couldn't think of anything I could have bought with a million bucks that would have given me half the pleasure of beating a bankruptcy rap."

He produced *A Night in Venice* in the 8,200-seat Marine Stadium at Jones Beach. "They said nobody would hold still for a Strauss operetta," he chortles. "They did. I gave 'em fireworks with it."

In 1950 he formed The Thomas-Todd Company with Lowell Thomas, the commentator, to experiment with a wide-screen process called Cinerama, and worked secretly on it for fourteen months. "The first time in my life I kept my mouth shut," he recalls proudly. He and Michael Junior shot eleven of the thirteen sequences for *This Is Cinerama,* including the historic roller-coaster ride.

It changed the face of the screen and, in two and a half years, grossed more than $20,000,000, an unheard-of record for a total of seventeen theaters.

Everyone associated with the venture was ecstatic, except Todd. He was dissatisfied with the necessity of three cameras, three projection machines and three separate strips of film that made imperfectly meshed images—and intimate scenes—impossible. "We can't stay on that roller-coaster and in the canals of Venice forever," he said. "Somebody has to say, 'I love you,' some day." A perfectionist and a realist, he was more interested in its failure than in its

success, as he was more interested in its future than in its present.

He sold out his interest to search beyond the horizon, to seek a process that would produce the effects of Cinerama with a single camera and film. He did, with the technical assistance of Dr. Brian O'Brien, the wizard of the University of Rochester and the American Optical Company.

The Todd-AO process was born. In the words of Dr. O'Brien, "Michael Todd was the first to recognize the need...and it is all due to his imagination. I am glad that the process has his name on it."

All this belongs to his Yesterday.

Around the World in 80 Days is his Today.

His Tomorrow? *Around the Solar System in 80 Minutes?*

Mike Todd widened the screen physically, now he intends to widen the vistas of expression upon it. To that end, he has, in this production, begun to bridge the motion picture medium and the theater.

It is only the beginning...

"I hate to be cryptic," he told me on his return from Moscow in May, 1956, "but I almost have something that can revolutionize all communication in the world. Let's see if I can explain it without telling you what it is." He reached for the telephone, next to his cigar, his favorite prop. "Say I suddenly got a terrific romantic urge. I'd just dial a number—and get sex over the phone. Would you call that revolutionary?"

"I would," I said.

He smiled and took a long, happy puff on his Romeo and Julieta DeLuxe No. 1 Dunhill Cedros, individually "selected and wrapped for Mr. Michael Todd."

A strange, quixotic fellow who has unconsciously dedicated his life to creating a legend of Mike Todd, a legend to conceal Avrom Goldbogen, a modest man, moral to the point of prudishness, the soul of gentleness and generosity, of whom his worst enemy could never say, "He was petty."

[Art Cohn, screen writer and author of *The Joker Is Wild,* is writing a biography of Mr. Todd.]

You Too Can Make a Picture!

No Previous Experience Necessary

DO IT YOURSELF

THANK GOODNESS everyone has two businesses. His own and show business. Everyone knows he can make a better picture than he saw last week. Why wait?

First, borrow, beg or *have* a few dollars and be certain there is nothing in all the world you want to buy except a few spools of tinted celluloid.

In Mike Todd's case, he unhesitatingly sold everything, including his interest in the Todd-AO process, his South African butterfly collection (*Lycaena icarus*), his membership in the Breakfast Club *and* Diners' Club, to make this show.

Next, select a subject that cannot be produced better on a 21-inch screen or by the I Will Arise Dramatic and Marching Club.

When Todd realized that to do *Around the World in 80 Days* right, he would need more than 68,894 people in thirteen different countries, he knew he had at last found something Ed Sullivan couldn't do, not in one installment anyway.

Then, cancel all bowling tournaments, barbecues and the Book-of-the-Month Club for two years. Four million air miles will have to be flown, 680,000 feet of color film will have to be shot, and, even with the advent of the horseless carriage, it takes time.

In the beginning, if you know your Bible, was the word.

Jules Verne, author, prophet and originator

of science fiction, wrote authoritatively about submarines, airplanes, rocket ships and television before they were invented, and minutely described the then astounding feat of going *Around the World in Eighty Days* without leaving his home in the French countryside. His fertile imagination was boundless: from the depths of *Thousand Leagues under the Sea* and *From the Earth to the Moon...to the Center of the Earth.*

"For the past twenty years," said Marshal Lyautey in 1905, when Verne died at the age of seventy-seven, "the advance of peoples is merely living the novels of Jules Verne."

Why do *80 Days?* Maybe you read it as a kid and it left a lasting impression. Maybe you figure almost everyone would like to go around the world, going to places or away from a place.

In Todd's case, it went back to 1946 when he started to produce a Broadway musical version of *80 Days* with a Cole Porter score and Orson Welles. Being superstitious, he insisted on reading a script; barely finishing same, he decided to withdraw from the project. First, he saw no percentage in sending more than 300,000 fresh dollars after the 40,000 he had already invested. Second, he had never produced a musical play that had run less than a year on Broadway and he did not want to break his luck. So he ran away to produce another day and, ten years later, made up his mind to get back the forty G's he had dropped, if it took X millions.

To adapt Verne's masterwork for the screen, you hire a writer. And a writer. And a writer. And a writer. You try an Englishman, a French-

man, an Irishman, a Gurkha too, until you find the right chemistry. His name is S. J. Perelman. One of America's top-drawer humorists, best known for his pieces in *The New Yorker,* Perelman wrote several motion picture comedies and, with his wife, collaborated on a play, *The Night Before Christmas,* concerning a gang of safecrackers who inadvertently tunnel into a delicatessen instead of a bank.

Strictly Mike Todd's kind of guy.

After you have the words on paper, you have to bring them to life. On this caper you will need *thirty-three* assistant directors, for it is one of the most complex productions ever attempted. So, if you're Todd, you will choose as your director a man just turned thirty-five who has never directed a picture in Hollywood and whose budgets for *all* the films he has made previously aggregated roughly the cost of shipping the cameras on this one. An Englishman named Michael Anderson.

Why shouldn't Todd pick a yearling like Anderson? It was Todd's first picture too. At least their mistakes would be new ones.

You are talking story to your director, and your man in charge of the budget breaks in to report that the accounting department needs more steel files — to handle the 8,100 payroll withholding forms.

"Eight thousand, one hundred payroll withholding forms!" you shout.

The man nods and, possibly for the first time, you realize you're in big business. And you need help.

You hire a man like William Cameron Menzies as associate producer. He's been around a long time; he wrote the book and he has a couple Academy Awards for bookends, one of them for *Gone with the Wind.*

You pick up a man here and a man there. Like Kevin O'Donovan McClory. You notice him while you are shooting in London: he is walking a little faster than the rest of the crew.

"Who is he?" you ask.

"The thirty-third assistant director," you are informed.

You move him up to thirty-second assistant director and take him to Paris. "Don't pack a

bag," you tell him. "You will be gone only one day."

You are ready to shoot the Paris sequence. "Who will volunteer for a raid against the enemy?" you ask, pointing to the 1955 cars that must be moved out of the street to play a scene in 1872.

An Irishman's voice speaks up. He continues to volunteer and you dispatch him to Pakistan, Siam, Hong Kong, Japan and points east.

In all, he flies 44, 535 miles around the world and then you take him to Hollywood to help edit the film. The week has stretched to more than a year, he still hasn't been home.

After the organization comes the cast.

You select the impeccable, urbane and imperturbable Britisher, David Niven, to play Phileas Fogg because he epitomized the public conception of Verne's classic adventurer. Then you get a brainstorm and decide on Mexico's beloved Cantinflas as his loyal valet. Madness? If you don't have such hot flashes and the courage to play them to the hilt—and, most important, are right—you should not be making *this* picture, a nice, safe "program" picture maybe.

"Cantinflas is the greatest living performer," says Todd. "Not only is he a magnificent actor and comedian, he's a noted bullfighter, musician, acrobat and can ride anything from a camel to a comet. Most important, he is essentially a pantomimist and will give the part true pathos. Get him."

"He can't be got," Todd's emissaries report a few weeks later. "Cantinflas is the wealthiest actor in the world, and the most independent. He has his own company, he has never made an American picture and, though he receives fabulous offers every week, he says he never will. More important, his manager, partner and closest friend, a man named Jacques Gelman, says

no. Gelman is tough."

Within a week, Cantinflas agreed to play the part, on a handshake with Todd. Gelman sealed the bargain by giving Mike a gold money clip encrusted with a rare Mexican coin.

How did he do it?

"Mr. Todd assured me the film would be done properly," explains Cantinflas, "and that I could portray Passepartout as a Latin. So, to my audience in Latin America, I'll still be Cantinflas."

Great casting calls for intuition, imagination and a magical gift to fuse human chemicals. One of the major problems was finding an actor to play the heavy, Inspector Fix, an obtuse man who believes he possesses shrewd cunning, a caricature of Hawkshaw and Javert, still *real*.

You choose Robert Newton, the gifted English actor. "This is my *best* part," he says. Ironically, it is also his last on this earth.

As the heroine, Princess Aouda, Todd wanted a new personality. He tested hundreds of girls in all parts of the world and settled for a red-headed Virginian who had not yet been in a film. Shirley MacLaine, an obscure dancer, has that whimsical, pixieish quality, you believe, that seems to fit into the chemistry of the other three characters traveling around the world.

Now you have the principals, all you have to do is fill in the small parts and you're set. But not if you're Mike Todd. To him there are no small parts, only small actors.

He proved it, the hard way, in his casting of

fifty "bit" parts that would appear on the screen only a few minutes, some but a few seconds. He made his point. There are no small roles in *80 Days* because he chose for each one an internationally famous actor deserving of his fame.

Todd calls them cameos, a word that is certain to enter the lexicon of show business.

A cameo, to Noah Webster, is "a gem carved in relief on stone."

A cameo, to Todd, is a gem carved in celluloid by a star.

"There have been many other pictures loaded with big names," he says, "but the story has always been built around the stars. My idea was to have each star fit the part in the story. Our story was about four people who go traveling. When you go traveling you meet a lot of people. It's that simple."

It's that simple—for Todd.

He talked Noel Coward into making his first American film appearance in twenty years, as the head of a London employment agency, for a single scene with Sir John Gielgud, one of the world's foremost Shakespearean actors. "Todd bullied me over an inferior lunch," recalls Coward, "and I gave in just for the devil of it."

It took Todd ten minutes, par for the course, to persuade Luis Miguel Domingúin, Spain's greatest living matador, to come out of retirement for a sequence.

"We forgot to mention money," Todd said as an afterthought when they shook hands.

"How much do you need?" asked the millionaire Domingúin.

A scene in a honky-tonk on San Francisco's Barbary Coast called for an anonymous piano player. Todd hired Frank Sinatra. "Not because he's Sinatra but because when he sits down at that piano with a bowler on his head and garters on his sleeve, he's for real. That's how I picked my people. They had to be for *real*."

Sinatra, Academy Award winner and the hottest actor in Hollywood, is seen for a brief flash and does not speak a word. With him in the same scene are Marlene Dietrich as a Tenderloin *femme fatale*, George Raft as a bouncer and Red Skelton as a drunk.

In the Paris sequence, Charles Boyer pops up as an ebullient clerk at Thomas Cook and Sons, and a pretty girl passing by is Martine Carol, France's leading actress. In Spain, José Greco performs a Gypsy dance and Gilbert Roland enters the scene as the potentate of a Moslem tribe. In India, Sir Cedric Hardwicke shows up as a stuffy brigadier general and Ronald Colman enters, fleetingly, as a railroad official.

"The face of Fernandel is as unforgettable as the Eiffel Tower," *Life* magazine observed. "It has helped to make him his country's greatest comic attraction." In *80 Days*, as a coachman in Paris, he speaks one word of dialogue.

John Mills, England's unforgettable star of *Great Expectations* and many other distinguished films, also bobs up as a cabby, in London, his brief speaking part restricted almost entirely to a series of hiccoughs.

The inimitable Beatrice Lillie, in private life

Lady Peel, the durable darling of two continents for more than thirty years, flashes swiftly across the screen as an evangelist who tries, with a street-corner sermon and a hymn, "Have courage, My Boy, to Say No!" to save the soul of Phileas Fogg.

Robert Morley, an outstanding British actor and playwright, remembered in London and on Broadway for countless roles, among them Oscar Wilde, and for *Edward, My Son*, in which he was the co-author as well as star, is cast as a governor of the Bank of England. Among his fellow members of the Reform Club, who wager Phileas Fogg that he cannot girdle the globe in eighty days, are Trevor Howard, the memorable star of *Brief Encounter* and *Outcast of the Islands;* Finlay Currie, a commanding figure on the English stage for more than fifty years; Basil Sydney, Ronald Squire and A. E. Matthews, each a great name in English drama.

Glynis Johns, Hermione Gingold and Evelyn Keyes turn up as tarts; Charles Coburn is a clerk in a Hong Kong steamship office; Joe E. Brown appears as a station-master at Fort Kearney and Buster Keaton as a railroad conductor. Colonel Tim McCoy (who else?) is a colonel of the U. S. Cavalry; Peter Lorre is a ship steward; Jack Oakie is captain of a merchant ship and his crew reunites the stars of *What Price Glory?* — Academy Award winner Victor McLaglen and Edmund Lowe — and Andy Devine.

"Todd never stopped talking," says one of his associates. "He sweet-talked the women and fast-talked the men, conning them into believing that only a real *top* name could afford to play a bit part and take alphabetical billing."

Todd dissents, "I didn't have to sell anybody, after we got rolling, My problem was keeping stars *out.*"

When the Screen Actors' Guild representative saw the first call sheet, he couldn't believe it. "Good heavens, Todd!" he exclaimed. "You've made extras of all the stars in Hollywood. There's no precedent for it."

He was to learn, as many have before him, that there is no precedent for almost everything Mike Todd does.

You have the stars, now you have to feed, dress, transport, house, rehearse and pamper them.

Start with the wardrobe. You have to design, make or rent 34,685 costumes in Spain, France, England, Japan, India, the Middle East and Hollywood. No use putting down how many tens of thousands of yards of material are necessary, or how many times they would circle the world, because you wouldn't believe it and it probably wouldn't be true either.

It was true, however, that Miles White, the costume designer, had to fly to Las Vegas three times to complete the fittings for one of those 34,685 costumes, a gown for Marlene Dietrich. It is true he had to whip up, ofttimes faster than you can say Passepartout, garments for a few thousand Orientals, a royal sari, tights for a wagonload of Barbary Coast belles, uniforms for a U. S. Cavalry, circa 1870, a coolie hat for the leading lady and a pair of pants to cover Andy Devine.

Item: 36,092 pieces of jewelry were needed.

Do you know what it means to dress, in period, a cast of some 6,400 Spaniards, 2,672 Japanese, 3,600 Moslems, 1,927 Arabs, 1,688 American Indians, 1,553 Englishmen and 1,664 Frenchmen — in their native lands — shooting a total of 160 days?

It was the biggest job ever given the Western Costume Company of Hollywood, the largest in America, in its forty year history, and Berman Ltd. of London. After its facilities were exhausted, Todd had to obtain additional costumes from Metro-Goldwyn-Mayer, Paramount, 20th Century-Fox, Warner Brothers, Universal-International and from the foremost English, Spanish and Oriental costume houses.

By now you have an army at your command.

You will have seventy make-up artists gluing beards on 15,612 chins. And they better be on the right chins. Heaven forbid a Vandyke is pasted where a Franz Joseph belongs or a zitz where there should be a Dundreary. Heads can roll.

You will order 97,463 yards of shawls hauled from Madrid to the town of Chinchon to decorate façades of 312 houses in a peaceful little town that you have converted into a bull ring.

You will use twenty airlines plus sixteen chartered planes.

You will rent 111 walkie-talkie phones from the U. S. Coast Guard and the Pakistan armies to keep in touch with your forces and, even in the town of Durango, Colorado (population 5,587), you will have four different telephone lines set up in your hotel suite. If you're Mike Todd, that is.

This is Big Time. You didn't plan it, it just turned out that way.

You have to make decisions every minute and they better make sense. It's your loot being burned up. You have 68,286 people, give or take a midget, on the payroll. And they all eat.

You finally start shooting—in 112 natural settings, on 140 sets that must be constructed, in 32 foreign locations, in 11 major studios.

If you're Todd, you go to Chinchon, Spain, and hire the *entire* population to play the parts of aficionados in the bullfight sequence. Unfortunately, they are insufficient to fill the huge bull ring, so you import hundreds of people daily and hope that no one will discern the difference between a true Chinchonian and an alien from Madrid.

Then you go to your good friend, the King of Thailand. He was grateful back in 1949 when you used his songs in *Peep Show*, and said if there was anything he could ever do to reciprocate, you must call on him.

You call on King Phumiphon and he insists on loaning you his royal barge, 165 feet long, complete with a solid gold throne and manned by seventy glitteringly clad oarsmen. He also sends along several units of the Royal Thailand Navy. You rehearse the oarsmen four months but it is worth it, they are on the screen all of twelve seconds.

You will need a Chinese dragon for your Hong Kong procession and you want the oldest and longest you can find. You settle for one 250 years old, thirty-six feet long, which requires twenty-four men to operate.

You hop over to the Persian Gulf and hire sixty Arabian dhows (don't betray your ignorance and admit you don't know that a dhow is a native vessel) from the Emir of Falaika, plus 450 Arabs to man them.

You move on to Pakistan with Kevin O'Donovan McClory and persuade the Nawab

of Pritim Pasha to loan you his private elephant herd of sixteen elephant boys for your jungle sequences. McClory makes a deal to spring for the boys' chow and the elephants', no more.

You better know the proper words when you have to hire 600 Moslems for a railroad station in Pakistan or cast Cheyennes, Apaches and Utes, 628 of them, for your American Indian sequences.

If you're Todd, you are a virtuoso on Indians and, on inspecting those 628 redskins at Durango, you know immediately that the Utes don't look enough like Indians. So every morning before you start shooting, you have them sprayed with a cosmetic dye, the precise red you wish. It will take fifty gallons of dye and it will be worth it.

If you're Todd, you are going first cabin and nothing is too minor for your personal attention, nothing too costly or too difficult to secure.

You want one of the greatest masterpieces of Buddhist art in Japan, the gigantic and beauti-

ful Great Buddha of Kamakura, forty-two feet high. You try to get it and can't. So you send your cast to it. What would Mohammed have done?

You want a real museum piece, a train that

ran from San Francisco to Colorado in 1871. You find it, diamond-stack engine and all, reposing in its place of honor in Brookside Park at Durango. Its owners refuse to lend it, but after weeks of persuasion, Todd-AO variety, plus a million-dollar bond that it will be returned in one piece, you get it on the road.

You will use 147 clocks and barometers of the nineteenth century in Phileas Fogg's London residence. Each one is authentic, as is the bell in the Lloyd's of London scene. This is the original bell — taken from the French frigate *Lutine* which went down in 1793—that is rung at Lloyd's every time that a disaster or an auspicious event occurs.

You must hire a corps of research and technical advisers to check on the authenticity of countless items...

Were there electric clocks in 1872? Yes. Were there telegraph wires in the United States that year? Yes. Were bets made at Lloyd's during the period? Indeed. There was enormous betting at Lloyd's during the nineteenth century, on all manner of things, orthodox and unorthodox. One underwriter would give odds on declaration of war with Spain or France on a given date, another actually offered "all newly married members one hundred to one against the contingency of twins."

Ad infinitum.

At last, after nearly a year of shooting, you have 680,000 feet of film—which must be cut and edited to 22,000 feet, approximately two hours and forty minutes on the screen.

Then comes the scoring. If you're Todd, you'll pick as your music master the man who has written such popular hits as "Sweet Sue," "Love Me Tonight" and "My Foolish Heart," and who has composed many of the most distinguished scores in the history of motion pictures, sufficient to be nominated personally for the Academy Award *twenty* times.

There are a few million other details, such as conceiving and executing a unique prologue that opens with the forgotten film of the first motion picture adapted from a Jules Verne story, *Rocket to Moon*, made in France more than sixty years ago and revealing, among other things, that such revolutionary devices as fade-outs were used before D. W. Griffith shot his first scene.

You will top this historical film with an exclusive, top-secret sequence of a guided missle, which cost a couple of million bucks to build, and from it the first shots ever seen eighty miles above the earth. You will persuade America's most distinguished commentator, Edward R. Murrow, to narrate this prologue. You will also create an animated epilogue, that for the first time makes it possible to sit through the seemingly endless credit titles, at the cost of a B picture—but who's watching the cash register?

Two or three other details remain, such as buying or leasing a theater in which to show the picture, advertising it and, of course, selecting the confections that will be sold in the lobby.

There now, wasn't it simple? Anyone can do it.

On second thought, don't memorize the details. Another picture might be different.

THE SCENE is LONDON, the London of Queen Victoria. London at its best, the serene glory of an English spring. Top hats glisten along the Row and parasols are the mode. London, the capital of an Empire that will never change. London of the fixed and invulnerable sterling.

A tall, elegantly attired gentleman, Phileas Fogg (David Niven), approaches the exclusive Reform Club, pauses and automatically takes out his watch and glances up. From his expression we knew this gesture only confirms the regularity of Big Ben. As he repockets his watch, his attention is diverted by a passing newsboy who carries a sandwich-board on which is emblazoned:

DAILY TELEGRAPH
BANK OF ENGLAND ROBBED

Along another street, a strange cycle — recently introduced from France, consisting of a large front wheel and an extremely small rear wheel — is propelled by an agile, wide-eyed, curiously dressed little man in a brown derby and patched, baggy pants, a Latin Don Juan of all trades called Passepartout (Cantinflas). He enters an employment agency where the proprietor (Noel Coward) is talking with a recently discharged gentleman's gentleman (Sir John Gielgud).

The subject of their animated discussion is Phileas Fogg, described by his ex-gentleman's gentleman as "a tyrant, a cold-hearted fiend, as cold and implacable as the two watches he carries about with him," whose bath water has to be exactly one foot three and a half inches, no less, no more, and whose morning toast has to be 83 degrees Fahrenheit, no more, no less.

It is impossible, it seems, to satisfy the exacting Mr. Fogg, as is attested by the five gentlemen's gentlemen he has run through in recent weeks via this agency alone. The proprietor's vexation is compounded by the fact that he knows no more about the enigmatic Mr. Fogg than he did before he supplied his first valet.

"He's not a professional man and he isn't in trade," he recapitulates. "He has apparently no family connections or background worth mentioning. He doesn't go in for hunting or fishing or, to coin a phrase, wenching. I cannot imagine how he ever got into the Reform Club!"

His reflection is interrupted by a soft Latin voice: "You have a nice little position for a gentleman's gentleman, sir?"

Thus Passepartout—trapeze artist, fireman, chimney sweep, et al—joins the service of Phileas Fogg.

That to-be-eventful night at the Reform Club begins no differently from any other night in its long past. This is a refuge where members can escape their wives and similar tedious obligations, dozing behind newspapers or sipping port.

A waiter replenishes a whisky-and-soda for a peer, and inquires, "Ice, your Lordship?"

"Certainly not! What do I look like—a polar bear?"

"Sorry, sir. Several of the members use it now and then."

Synopsis of S. J. Perelman's Adaptation of
Jules Verne's
Around the World
in Eighty Days

"Learned it from some Yankee, I dare say. Those redskins over there drink anything."

"Dangerous custom, I've always thought, sir," the waiter agrees. "A man could catch a nasty chill on his liver."

"Or break a tooth! Remind me to speak to the House Committee — no, by gad, I'll write a letter to the *Times!*"

In the card room, Fogg is playing with his customary trio of partners at whist and two other members look on, all weighty and influential folk. One of them, a Governor of the Bank of England (Robert Morley), is the pompous butt of facetious barbs inspired by the bold robbery of £55,000 from under the nose of his head cashier.

"Surely," comments one of them (Trevor Howard), "you've some better hiding place for your funds than a cashier's nose."

"Go ahead and jeer, gentlemen," says the Governor, "but I promise you, we'll lay the culprit by the heels soon enough. We've notified detectives all over the shop, from Liverpool to Cairo, and circulated a full description throughout Europe and America. He won't get very far."

Fogg quietly suggests that the bank robber is a rather exceptional person and should not be underestimated: only a cool and logical man could have engineered such an exploit or gained access to a vault that had been considered impregnable. "Obviously a gentleman, and one with considerable presence of mind."

The Governor eyes Fogg suspiciously. "You seem to know more about this affair than the police," he says.

"Merely what one would deduce from the facts," says Fogg, reaching for the cards. "Our trick, Flanagan."

This touches off a discussion on the odds for and against a resourceful thief. There are plenty of places to hide, one comments, the world's a pretty large affair.

"It was, a hundred years ago, it isn't any longer," the Governor insists. "You can girdle the entire globe today in three months."

"In less than that, to be precise," Fogg interjects softly. "In eighty days."

The others look at him as if he were bereft of his senses. He cannot be serious. "Around the world in eighty days? It's inconceivable, it's

impossible!"

"Nothing is impossible," says Fogg. "When science finally conquers the air, it may be feasible to circle the world in eighty hours."

His listeners dismiss this as a beautiful chimera but hold him to his original claim: that the world can be circled in eighty days. Even if one made ideal connections at every point, one of them contends, there would still be typhoons, shipwrecks, unforeseen delays such as being waylaid by brigands or struck by an avalanche or falling into a chasm.

"I include the unforeseen," says Fogg. "My estimate makes full provision for chasms."

One word leads to another, Fogg is challenged to back up his boast and, to make it worth his while and theirs, one wagers him five thousand pounds that he is wrong. The others are equally eager to bet.

Fogg covers all their wagers, to the tune of twenty thousand pounds that he has on deposit at Baring's Bank.

"If my memory is correct," says Fogg, "the boat train for Dover leaves London Bridge Station at a quarter before nine tonight. I shall be on it."

The others look at him incredulously. How can a man start out on a trip around the world without a few days to settle his affairs and make preparations?

"I'm quite ready now," says Fogg. "Let's recapitulate. Today is Wednesday, the second of October. I engage to be back here in London, in the card room of the Reform Club, on Saturday the twenty-first of December at a quarter before nine P.M. I shall post my cheque for twenty thousand pounds beside yours at the conclusion of this rubber." He permits himself a wintry smile. "And now, gentlemen, I believe diamonds are trumps. Let us finish our game."

As the imperturbable Mr. Fogg focuses his undivided attention on his cards, his five fellow members regard him with varying degrees of awe and stupefaction.

Their first stop is Paris. Fogg nearly loses Passepartout at the Gare du Nord to a pretty girl (Maritine Carol), whom he pretends to recognize as a "cousin." A ringing slap across the face informs Passepartout that they are not related, nor will there be any relationship.

A horse-faced cabman (Fernandel) takes them in his fiacre to Thomas Cook & Sons, where Fogg learns that an avalanche has sealed the Montfort railroad tunnel to Marseilles, that all roads are blocked, and that nothing will get through for at least a week. Fogg meets his first emergency with characteristic aplomb. "There must be some other way," he says resolutely.

"But we are not birds, Master," says Passepartout. "We cannot fly across the mountains."

"That is not unfeasible, Monsieur, fantastic as it seems," says the dapper Frenchman (Charles Boyer) who has been charting their itinerary. He produces a card bearing a reproduction of a gaily painted balloon. "I have made sixty-three ascents, gentlemen," he says, "many of them to an elevation of a thousand meters."

"You're quite sure this is not just Gallic braggadocio?" Fogg inquires doubtfully.

"Monsieur," the agent says, striking a pose worthy of Napoleon, "you are addressing the second most celebrated balloonist in Europe." Under Fogg's questioning he reveals that the first most celebrated balloonist was buried the day before.

Fogg commands Passepartout to open the carpetbag. He hands over a bundle of fresh banknotes and is the owner of a balloon.

The balloon in 1872 was a gay sight, particularly a balloon made in Paris. Colors in all shapes and design decorate the huge silk bag. A crowd has gathered in the countryside near Paris to wish Fogg bon voyage.

While a small band plays, and a photographer takes pictures, and Fogg, already in the basket, receives a hamper of food and other gifts, Passepartout kisses a pretty mademoiselle here and there, and quite blissful about it all, pulls a loose rope and accidently releases the balloon. Only through some fancy gymnastics is he able to get aboard as it surges upward.

Sailing sublimely across the sky, Fogg and Passepartout, a remarkable pair, remarkably attired, Fogg in his high straw hat and long gray coat, his valet in his brown derby and patched, baggy pants, scan the French country-side as it rolls below them — the outskirts of Paris in the early morning, Sacre Coeur, the lush gardens of the Tuileries, castles, vineyards, chateaux, and the patchwork of farms along the River Seine.

The scene changes and they leave the verdant valleys for the snow-capped summits. As they approach a mountain crag powdered with snow, Passepartout snatches a handful of ice, pops it into a champagne bucket and proceeds to cool a bottle he is preparing for Fogg's lunch. From the hamper he extracts a chicken and hands his master a succulent leg. When the champagne is properly iced, he pours two glasses and, drifting across the Alps, he and his master toast each other and their voyage.

In London, one of the members who has covered Fogg's wager bursts into the Reform Club flourishing a copy of the *Morning Telegraph.* "Gentlemen, I think this calls for a restrained celebration," he says jubilantly. "Guess what's become of our intrepid Mr. Fogg! He's drifting over the Alps in a balloon!"

The Governor of the Bank of England is aghast. "Jiggery-pokery, sir," he says, "what would he be doing in one of those?"

The others comment that he had failed to mention the use of a balloon, it was not very sporting of him, a bit on the sly side.

"Seems quite resourceful to me," says a dissenter. "English ingenuity—never say die—and all that sort of thing."

The Governor's face darkens. "Does the paper mention which Alps he's drifting over?" he asks.

"Why—er—no," stammers the no-longer jubilant news bearer. "I assume the ones in Switzerland."

The Governor glares at him. "Indeed, refer to your atlas," he says scathingly. "It could also be the Maritime Alps, in the South of France, in which case Fogg is not only on schedule but *ahead* of it! What were you saying about a celebration, sir?"

The balloon drifts across the countryside. Beyond, in the full beauty of the late afternoon sun, we see an ancient walled town nestling crescent-like by the blue sea. Yellow bastions, weathered rooftops and ancient churches thrust skyward. The crescent is lined with a neat, unruffled fringe of white sand. Fishing boats are anchored and are drawn up on the beach.

Fogg snaps shut his telescope. "The southern perimeter of France, Passepartout, often justifiably referred to in the guide books as the Azure Coast. I think the moment is propitious for our descent." He takes hold of the valve line. "It's really quite simple. We empty out some sand and we go up. We pull this and with any luck we come down. I imagine we release some gas from the top of the balloon."

"Gas!" Passepartout cries out in dismay. "I forgot to turn off the gas in my room."

"It doesn't matter," says Fogg. "It'll continue to burn—at your expense." He tugs on the valve line which apparently has become jammed. Passepartout scrambles upward into the rigging like the expert acrobat he is, at last releases the valve line and the balloon sinks earthward.

On the ground, to their astonishment, they learn that they are not in France but have drifted to Spain, requiring a long roundabout train journey to Marseilles. Further inquiry discloses that the trip can be made by sea in a fast boat in ten hours—but only one such craft is in the harbor, the yacht of Abdullah Achmed of Tangiers. That worthy, they learned, sleeps by day and spends his nights in the Cave of the Seven Winds.

Passepartout knows, by the glint in Phileas Fogg's eye, that he means to get Abdullah Achmed's yacht, whatever the cost.

The Castilian tavern called the Cave of the Seven Winds reverberates to the click-clack of castanets, the strumming of guitars, the clapping of hands, rich voices lifted in song and laughter and the staccato beat of beautiful and handsome Gypsies dancing the flamenco, led by the incomparable José Greco.

In the enthusiastic crowd sits Passepartout, his Latin blood boiling happily from the wine, the women and the wild rhythms. His elegant, imperturbable master is, of course, aloofly interested.

The theme of the dance number is a bullfight and, no longer able to control his emotions, Passepartout springs to his feet, seizes a red tablecloth, which he converts into a cape, and executes a series of spirited and graceful passes with a gorgeous Gypsy girl playing the bull.

The tavern rings with *"Olés!"* until Fogg puts an end to the nonsense and comes to the business at hand: securing, for the next lap of their race against time and a £20,000 wager — around the world in eighty days — the only craft available to take them to Marseilles, the yacht of Abdullah Achmed.

The potentate (Gilbert Roland), seated with his entourage of fierce-eyed men in flowing turbans and white robes, with gleaming knives dangling from their waists, listens to Fogg's request and grants him the use of the yacht, gratis, on condition that Passepartout, whose cape-work on the dance floor he has admired, will give another exhibition — the following day in the bull ring.

"But it would be a massacre!" Fogg protests.

"Let me, Master," Passepartout pleads. "I am not afraid."

The bull ring is filled with aficionados, at-

tracted by the appearance of their greatest matador (Luis Miguel Domingúin) and an alien buffoon who has struck the fancy of their potentate, who is flanked by his court, and Mr. Fogg, in the royal box.

The famed matador finishes his bull and tosses his cape carelessly to Passepartout, who presents a pathetic sight in a borrowed outfit of which the brocade is faded and the pants too large. Across the seat is an enormous rip, the mark of the horn that finished its previous owner. "You're next," says the matador.

Passepartout thrusts the cape to another matador. "You're next," he quavers.

The matador gestures and, in a moment, Passepartout is being propelled by several powerful arms into the ring. "Please," he protests, shaking and struggling, "I'm not in the mood. I mean, the bull's not in the mood... We wouldn't be happy together—his horns are not my size."

The bull faces Passepartout and is intrigued. The raffish little man makes a brave pass with his cape; then, heartened by his success, continues to improvise. Every movement is unorthodox and the bull is bewildered. Not even a bull can give Passepartout an inch. It is the beginning of the end—for el toro. A matter of time before Passepartout is carried triumphantly around the ring on admiring shoulders, the air filled with flowers tossed by fair señoritas. Wine skins rain down...

Achmed Abdullah turns to Fogg. "My ship is at your disposal, sir. If you leave now, you will arrive in Marseilles in ten hours."

All goes well until Suez, colorful gateway from the Mediterranean to the Far East. As Passepartout descends the gangplank of R.M.S. Mongolia and reports with papers to customs, a gimlet-eyed man with an authoritative air, devoid of uniform or official badge, blocks Passepartout. "Where is the gentleman who owns this passport—this Mr.—er—Phileas Fogg?"

"My master is staying on board."

The questioner, an adhesive and implacable private sleuth named Inspector Fix (Robert Newton), is instantly on the qui vive. "Indeed. Well, he'll have to report in person to the British Consulate to establish his identity."

Passepartout asks if it is necessary. "Not necessary," says Mr. Fix. "Mandatory!"

Passepartout shrugs in resignation and goes up the gangway. Fix waits until he disappears and then follows. Behind a potted palm in the dining saloon, Mr. Fix watches Passepartout go to his master. The gleam of a triumphant hunter invades Mr. Fix's eyes as he compares Mr. Fogg's appearance with the description which he holds in his hand.

On the wharf, Mr. Fix overtakes Passepartout and, with great affability, engages him in conversation. Passepartout naively answers his leading questions. Yes, they left London hastily. "Like a shot. Forty-five minutes after he told me — zut! — we're off around the world. From one end to the other within eighty days. He says it's a wager, but between you and me, I don't believe a word of it."

Mr. Fix's eyes narrow. "Something else in the wind, eh? I understand he gave the officers of the *Mongolia* a bonus to get the ship here ahead of time. He must be a very rich man."

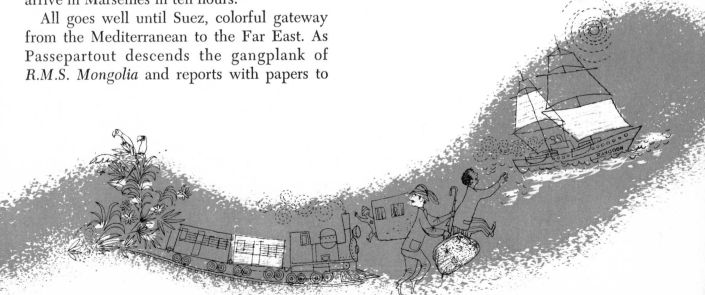

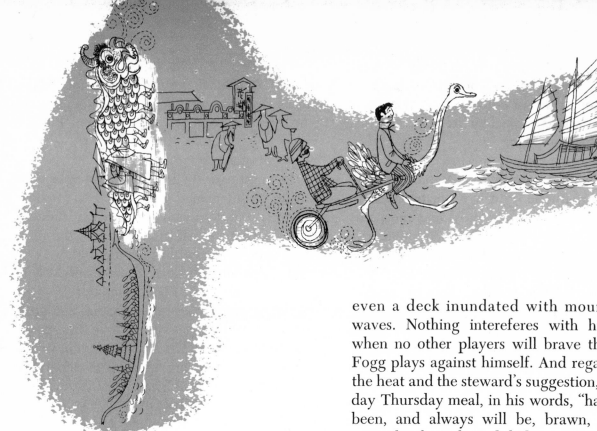

Passepartout drinks in the adulation. "You should see how much money we carry with us," he whispers confidentially. "All in brand-new banknotes."

Inspector Fix scurries to Her Majesty's consul. But Fogg has already been there before him, with his credentials all in order.

Fix hands a paper to the official. "Here is the description of the man who robbed the Bank of England."

The consul shakes his head. "It tallies exactly!" he admits. "What do you propose to do?"

Inspector Fix chortles. "Notify London to send a warrant to Bombay, accompany Fogg there, and arrest him the moment he sets foot on British soil."

"Very enterprising of you, Fix," responds the consul teasingly. "Nice sea voyage at the expense of Scotland Yard—what?"

"I beg your pardon, sir," says Inspector Fix austerely. "I see my duty and I do it."

Aboard ship, enroute from Suez to Bombay, life for Fogg is comparatively little different than if he were ensconced in the comfort of his home on Savile Row or in his favorite chair at the exclusive Reform Club.

Come glassy sea or typhoon, his tea must be served at the stroke of four P.M., on deck,

even a deck inundated with mountainous waves. Nothing intereferes with his whist; when no other players will brave the storm, Fogg plays against himself. And regardless of the heat and the steward's suggestion, his midday Thursday meal, in his words, "has always been, and always will be, brawn, Windsor soup, beef steak and kidney pie, roly-poly pudding, Stilton cheese, and a glass of vintage wine."

Aboard, unknown to Fogg, is the detective, Inspector Fix, who, convinced by circulars of identification that Fogg is wanted for the robbery of the Bank of England, has wired Scotland Yard for a warrant to arrest him the moment he touches British soil.

The warrant is not waiting at Bombay and no amount of pleas, threats—or an offer to divide the reward of £2,000—can persuade the police inspector (Reginald Denny) to arrest Fogg.

At the railroad station, Fogg impatiently paces the platform as the train prepares to depart for Calcutta. "Devil take the man. Where can he be?" he asks, searching for his valet Passepartout, who has gone to purchase gear for their journey through the jungle.

"Panting after some woman or other, I suppose," responds a fellow traveler, Sir Francis Cromarty, a brigadier-general in the English Army (Sir Cedric Hardwicke). "These foreigners, you know."

Passepartout, never one to take a straight line between two points, has improved the last hour or two badgering a Brahma bull. He uses his jacket as a matador's cape, unaware that he is teasing a sacred animal. Infuriated Hin-

dus take after him, chasing him through the narrow passageways into the temple of Hanuman, the Monkey God. The priests feeding the sacred monkeys are, naturally, horrified at the sight of an unbeliever loose in the tabernacle, and especially one who has neglected to remove his shoes.

Pursued by a throng of outraged priests and barking dogs, Passepartout manages to scramble aboard the train, already under way, only by grasping the handle of Fogg's outstretched umbrella.

The colorful journey into the interior, past herds of elephants and native craft poling upstream, and Fogg's whist game with Sir Francis, is interrupted by the sudden halt of the train in the thick of the jungle. It is the end of the line, they learn to their consternation from a passing official (Ronald Colman). Fifty miles of track remain to be laid to Allahabad.

Fogg, unlike Sir Francis, is composed. "I knew some obstacle would arise en route," he explains, "and I thriftily gained two extra days crossing the Arabian Ocean. A steamer leaves Calcutta for Hong Kong at noon the twenty-fifth. Our only problem is to find some means of conveyance to Allahabad."

The means turns out to be a huge elephant, which goes crashing through the bush with Mr. Fogg, Passepartout and Sir Francis rocking in a howdah slung on its back.

That night, huddled around a tiny campfire, their elephant boy, Paku, suddenly stamps out and scatters the embers. Sir Francis silences Fogg's protest as a dissonant chant, a clashing of cymbals and a tinkling of bells herald a religious procession. It moves along the bank of the river, illuminated by the light of a hundred torches.

Fogg peers through the bushes and sees a group of native porters carrying a litter. On it is Princess Aouda (Shirley MacLaine), young and beautiful and sadly resigned. She wears a magnificent sari, bordered with gold, and her head and arms are aflame with jewels. Behind her come guards with naked sabers and damascened pistols, bearing another litter. On it is the corpse of an old rajah wearing, as in life, a turban of pearls and a scarf of cashmere sewn with diamonds.

It is a "suttee," Sir Francis explains, a voluntary human sacrifice in which a wife is burned on the funeral pyre of her husband.

"Forgive me, Sahib," Paku interjects, "but the lady does not wish to commit suttee. She is being forced—out of custom." Fogg's interest mounts. "Aouda very fine person," Paku goes on. "Very beautiful, very...she was educated in England!"

"That decides it," says Fogg, and turns to Sir Francis. "General, we place ourselves under your command."

Sir Francis puts spyglass to eye and scans the situation. Below is a delicately minaretted pagoda. In front of it stands a tall funeral pyre of wood, stacked neatly, gleaming with oil. The porters place the litter with the rajah's corpse atop it.

"Devilish!" Sir Francis growls sotto voce. "Guards are posted about the temple. Can't seem to find an opening."

"And the princess?" Fogg asks anxiously.

"Inside—completely surrounded by armed men...Simple! We'll *flank* the beggars!" Using his swagger stick, he draws a map on the ground. "Now, then. Here's the temple. There's the funeral pyre. We create a diversionary action here...make a sortie there...and enfilade their guards from the rear."

"But we're only four of us all told," Fogg reminds him.

"Exactly." Sir Francis nods emphatically. "It can't possibly work with less than seventy-five men. Speaking as a strategist, sir, I'd say our position is untenable."

"Nevertheless, whatever the odds..." Fogg stops. Passepartout is gone.

Below, priests and guards carry the protesting form of Princess Aouda to the pyre, where she is placed, still struggling, alongside the figure of the rajah. The weird music increases as a priest applies the torch and the pyre bursts into flame.

There is an awful hush from the crowd. Suddenly...

The figure of the rajah sits up slowly. It rises stiffly, picks up the bride, and strides through the smoke and flames. Princess Aouda looks at its shrouded face and swoons.

The priests, the fakirs, the fanatics, the guards, and relatives fall to the ground, hiding their faces before this Lazarus returned from the dead.

Through the supine mob strides the figure of the rajah, stepping on backs and outflung hands. One end of his turban hangs loose, begins to unwind. Suddenly the whole thing falls off and we recognize Passepartout.

Paku is waiting at the kneeling elephant, Fogg and Sir Francis covering them with their guns.

Princess Aouda, trembling, falls to her knees. "Gentlemen, you have rescued me. All my life..."

"Madame, the moment is hardly opportune for gratitude," says Fogg. "Allow me to help you."

He hoists her to the howdah and clambers on himself, with the others, as Paku guides the great beast into the jungle at a rapid trot.

A bit of unpleasantness at Calcutta, Fogg's arrest for abduction of an Indian princess, is left in the wake of the ship. He posts bail and shrugs off the incident.

The exotic East of Siam unfolds...

Now the elegant Fogg and the lovely Aouda stand at the railing gazing over the placid sea and the setting sun. He is talking, as usual, about whist. "I finessed my queen of hearts and forced Finch-Tattersall to sacrifice his ace. Poor fellow went dead white—bit right through his pipe-stem. Oh, well...I'm afraid I've bored you."

"How can you say that," Mr. Fogg?" she asks sincerely. "That's the most enthralling

story I've ever heard! There's a kind of precision about whist. I've always admired men who were precise..."

Fogg turns to her with new interest and the rapport becomes greater when she discloses that she met the late rajah only once—at the age of seven, before her parents sent her to England to be educated. She was his wife in name only.

Fogg, enraptured, regards her with new interest. "Aouda..." he says softly, "would you care to hear about the time I drew a flush hand in diamonds."

"If you'd care to confide in me," she replies.

Later she asks Passepartout if his master is always so proper and formal. "Have there been any women in his life?"

"I assume he must have had a mother," he replies, "but I am not certain."

Inspector Fix has been busy. He learns from the chief steward that Fogg has made reservations on the S.S. *Carnatic* to Yokohama the morning after they arrive in Hong Kong. "That gives me twenty hours," says Fix. "I'll tag the blighter there if I have to turn out the

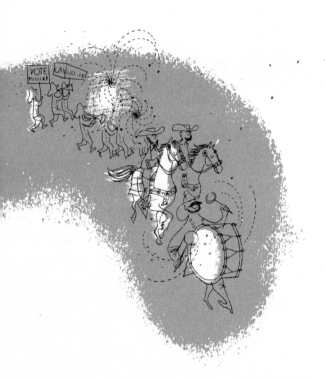

Governor to do it."

They land in noisy, bustling Hong Kong and Fogg hails rickshaws for Aouda, Passepartout and himself.

Inspector Fix arrives a moment later, addresses an idling coolie and points after Fogg. "Follow that rickshaw!"

Fogg escorts Princess Aouda to the Royal Club Hotel and, extracting a sheaf of crisp banknotes from his bottomless carpetbag, dispatches Passepartout to secure three cabins aboard the *Carnatic*. "And no dilly-dally," Fogg commands.

"No dilly-dally," says Passepartout and takes off on an ostrich.

A moment later, Inspector Fix arrives at the ostrich stand. He points to the fleeting Passepartout, gets astride a tethered bird, and shouts, "Follow that ostrich!"

Fix catches up with Passepartout at the steamship ticket office. "Well, sink me if it isn't my old friend off the *Rangoon,*" the Inspector exclaims. Then he pretends to be inspired. "Since we may not see each other again," he suggests, "why don't we have a little farewell drink?" Passepartout declines.

"For old lang syne, former shipmates, that sort of thing," Fix implores. Passepartout weakens.

Fogg and Aouda, meantime, are discovering each other further. "I'm afraid I must be a burden to you," she says.

"Quite the reverse," he says gallantly. "Your company has been most welcome."

"I only wish I could express my infinite gratitude," she says, attempting to kiss his hand.

"Please," he says, withdrawing sharply. "You really shouldn't do that sort of thing."

"Oh, Mr. Fogg! Why must you be so—so British?"

"Madame, I am what I am," he says with cold formality.

"No—you're—kind—and warm—and generous."

After a constrained pause he offers her his arm. "Would you care to join me on the veranda? I understand they serve an outstanding lemon squash."

At this moment, Passepartout too is ordering a squash, in a dark and murky waterfront dive, but Inspector Fix countermands it. "Poppycock! I said I'd buy you a drink, not a blooming tonic." He turns to the waiter with a significant wink. "My friend and I will have a Hong Kong Snickersnee."

While they were waiting for the drinks, Fix confides in Passepartout; he is a professional detective in pursuit of Fogg, wanted for robbing the Bank of England of £55,000 sterling. Passepartout is enraged and believes not a word.

"The description tallies in every respect,"

says Fix. "This flight around the world is a ruse to dupe those idiots in London. I wasn't going to tell you this—but why be greedy?" He lowers his voice intimately: "There's plenty for *both* of us: two thousands pounds and five percent of the monies recovered. What do you say? Think you'd like to split a little nestegg with me?"

Passepartout is too stunned to respond.

"Just help me delay Fogg twenty-four hours till my warrant arrives," Fix beggs.

Passepartout, furious, starts to rise. "You think I'd betray Mr. Fogg?"

Fix forces him down. "All right, all right, you needn't get angry. Shows you're a loyal and trustworthy chap. I respect that. Let's have a little libation on the altar of friendship." Passepartout refuses but Inspector Fix appeals to his forgiving nature and clinks glasses. "Here! Confusion to the enemies of the Crown..."

Passepartout wrestles with his conscience; at last he takes a gulp, becomes rigid. His eyes roll back and he passes out, cold. Fix claps his hands; a pair of strong coolies lift the valet from the floor and tote him out into the shadows of the wharves.

He comes to in a cabin on the S.S. *Carnatic*, en route to Yokohama, but Fogg and Princess Aouda are not aboard. Passepartout reaches into his pockets and wilts: his money is gone, as are the other two steamship tickets.

"The police, they find you with one ticket in pocket, carry you here," the steward (Peter Lorre) informs him. "You sleep like baby."

"Oh," Passepartout groans. "I have betrayed my master. Everything is lost..."

Note quite. The resourceful Mr. Fogg, distressed by the mysterious disappearance of Passepartout, has chartered a three-masted Chinese junk with red sails which will bring him into Yokohama a day later than the *Carnatic* but in time to catch the *President Grant* for San Francisco. Inspector Fix entreats him to let him go along—"to visit an ailing cousin, Marmaduke, in San Francisco"—and Fogg innocently welcomes him aboard.

Passepartout wanders about Yokohama, famished, penniless, disconsolate...

The stalls are loaded with trays of succulent sea food and poultry. Passepartout's hunger and misery mount. He shuffles toward a theater with a sign: CIRQUE—CIRCUS.

It is a spectacular circus: death-defying acrobats, amazing magicians, tightrope walkers, fire-eaters, flame-throwers...

Arriving in Yokohama, after an extended search, Fogg finds his valet at last. "Passepartout!" he calls out.

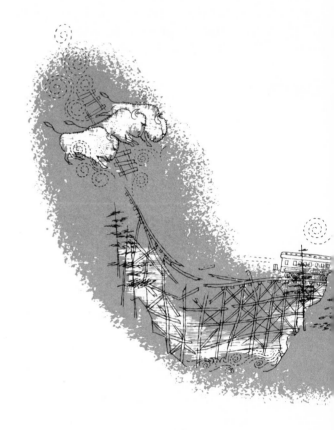

Passepartout, in flowing Japanese robe, turns his head. "Master!" he screams joyfully, and dashes from the stage where he has been supporting ten acrobats. The pyramid collapses with the departure of its base; the top man desperately reaches for and clutches a rope above—the curtains come tumbling with the men, the show is ruined, and the audience is in panic.

Passepartout is oblivious of the havoc. He is reunited with his master.

San Francisco is in the frenzy of a turbulent

political campaign, this summer of 1872, the sky afire with fireworks, the streets festooned with flags and banners and clogged with bands, Zouaves, partisans, orators and horse-drawn brewery wagons with enormous kegs, on which sit beautiful spangled girls from the Barbary Coast, waving banners, and throwing kisses to the crowd.

Fogg, offended by the sight of ladies exhibiting their shapely legs so casually, takes off his

hat to shield Princess Aouda's eyes.

"Please let me watch," she begs, pushing the hat aside. "These native customs fascinate me."

"Is this a religious spectacle?" Passepartout asks.

A cadaverous candidate with long mustaches, a long black cigar and figured vest, approaches with free cigars. This is Colonel Stamp Proctor (John Carradine). Fogg declines his proffered stogie. "I happen to prefer the brand my tobacconist compounds for me," he explains.

"Well, sweet spirits of nitre, aren't you the tender bud? Tell me, Percy, how are you voting? Camerfield or Mandiboy?"

For neither, Fogg responds. He is a foreign visitor and quite unconcerned which of the two triumphs.

"I'll be a ring-tailed side-winder if you don't raise my gorge," storms the Colonel. "Yes siree bob, I'll be a dad-burned polecat if you aren't as ornery a specimen as I ever clapped eyes on!" He reaches for Aouda's sari. "And what kind of foreigner are you—a hootchy-kootchy dancer?"

"Unhand that lady, sir!" commands Fogg.

"Lah-de-dah! Why don't you make me?" Colonel Proctor taunts him.

"I shall, sir, without further invitation." Fogg brings his trusty umbrella down on the Colonel's head, creasing the latter's ten-gallon hat. The Colonel swings, Fogg ducks and the blow catches Inspector Fix in the eye. Fogg hits the Colonel in the foot with the ferrule of his umbrella. Proctor lets out a yell and grabs Fogg by the necktie. Before he can commit any damage, Fogg delivers a second successful blow with his umbrella on the Colonel's head. The Colonel goes down and out.

Passepartout drifts into a honky-tonk where a drunk (Red Skelton) stuffs himself from the free-lunch counter, filling his gullet, pockets and hat with chicken, eggs, sea food and other morsels until the bouncer (George Raft) collars him and heaves him outside into the gutter.

Fogg comes in looking for Passepartout, and is stopped by a Barbary Coast *femme fatale* (Marlene Dietrich). She invites him to tarry at her table but their conversation is interrupted by a stiletto expertly hurled by the bouncer, which misses Fogg by inches. Fogg needs no further prodding. He gathers up Passepartout and Aouda and leaves; the pianist (Frank Sinatra), in a bowler hat and sleeve garters, never misses a beat.

Crossing the rugged frontier of the Rockies against time, with a wager of £20,000 hanging on the outcome, taxes Phileas Fogg's resourcefulness and fortitude.

There are all manner of stops not indicated on the railroad timetable; a herd of buffalo delays the train for nearly an hour before it crosses the tracks.

The ancient engine, belching smoke from its diamond stack, chugs through the mountainous country, at last reaches a bridge some of whose foundations have been washed away by flood waters. The tracks are crooked and hang like wet ropes. The engineer stops the train and goes out to survey the situation. "The bridge won't support the locomotive," he announces. The fireman agrees.

Colonel Proctor, who is aboard, lets out a roar of protest. "What the tarnation's wrong with all you lily-livered, snivelin' chaw-bacons? Hang me for a sheep-stealin' son of a tarantula if you ain't a pack of yellow-bellied milksops!" He extracts a flask of whisky from a capacious pocket and thrusts it into the engineer's hand. "Take a snort of this forty-rod. Back up your old teakettle and shoot her over at thirty miles an hour!"

Fortified, the engineer sends the train flying across and, as the last car gets across, the bridge disintegrates and falls—rails, ties, trestles and all—with a thunderous roar into the abyss.

Colonel Proctor struts triumphantly into the passenger car where Fogg is playing whist with Aouda against Inspector Fix and Passepartout. "Why don't you play an American game, you swabs?" he goads them. "Red Dog! Euchre! Want me to learn you how, Algy boy? Or shall I learn you how to fight fair, you yellow-bellied lime-juicer?"

"Sir," says Fogg, looking up, "you are an insolent bully and I demand satisfaction at once."

The conductor (Buster Keaton) obliges them and leads them to another car where they can wage their duel, first hustling out the occupants. Fogg and Colonel Proctor stand in the middle of the car, backs touching, each holding a large six-shooter. Each marches, on count, to the opposite ends of the car. The Colonel turns, sights his gun at Fogg's head and...

Before he can squeeze the trigger, there is a crash of glass and an arrow transfixes his shoul-der. "Injuns!" he screams.

Fogg pulls the arrow from the Colonel's shoulder then jams a handkerchief in the wound. "Thanks, partner," gasps the Colonel. "You may be a foreigner, but you're true blue."

An enormous band of Indians, shooting arrows and guns, waving tomahawks and whooping in properly bloodthirsty manner, converge on the train, many leaping from the saddles.

Fogg fires in all directions and several redskins bite the dust, not one an instant too soon.

"Fort Kearney's just ahead," gasps the conductor as an arrow drives between his shoulder blades. "That's where the Cavalry is…"

The train careens wildly and for sufficient reason: the engineer and firemen have been killed and an Indian is trying to operate the controls. Passepartout, scrambling atop the cars, leaps upon him and swings the balance of power back to the palefaces.

Later that day, Fogg, Aouda and Fix reach the Fort Kearney station but Passepartout is missing. "No sign of your man, sir," the Captain of the Cavalry (Captain Tim McCoy) tells Fogg. "I'm afraid he's fallen into the hands of the Sioux."

At Fogg's plea, the Captain organizes a raid and, with Fogg at his side, goes in pursuit of the Indians. In an epic chase between white man and redskin, they ride and fight their way to the Sioux encampment.

On a rack, surrounded by Indians capering in a barbaric war dance, Passepartout is visible, shackled and terrified. The Chief applies a torch to the twigs around him, and tongues of flame leap up about the captive's body.

Passepartout prays in his native tongue. The Indians circle around him, howling.

There is a shrill bark of a bugle and, over the brow of yon summit sweeps the righteous, wrathful might of the United States Cavalry, led by the Captain and—of course—Phileas Fogg, his jaw set, his silk hat cocked against the wind.

Passepartout's eyes widen, his face flooded with joy and relief. "Master!" he screams.

Back at the depot, Fogg's party sit lugubriously on a baggage wagon. "No use bein' blue, folks," says the stationmaster (Joe E. Brown). "A local comes through here tomorrow and that'll fetch you into Omaha the next day."

"And we'll miss our steamship at New York," says Fogg dejectedly. "How do we get to Liverpool on schedule?"

As he speaks, he feels the breath of a breeze. Across the tracks his eyes spot a medicine wagon, the light wind flapping its canvas cover. Fogg's eyes move along the track—to a number of rusting railway wheels and axles, spare parts. He wets his finger and holds it to the wind.

Not long after, Fogg, Aouda, Passepartout and Fix are sailing along on their baggage wagon, which has been converted into a land yacht, the cover acting as a sail. It rolls smoothly across the wind-tossed prairie sea, every click on the rails bringing Phileas Fogg closer to his beloved England.

Prospects have brightened for the five members of London's exclusive Reform Club who wagered Fogg £20,000 sterling he could not girdle the globe in eighty days. They have confirmation by cable that Fogg has missed his liner from New York. There is no other eastbound vessel which could bring him into Liverpool in time to collect his bet.

"May as well broach that bottle of champagne we've been saving," one of them suggests exultantly. Another demurs. "First let's place a side bet or two before this information leaks out."

The Governor of the Bank of England, accompanied by an inspector of Scotland Yard, finds them at Lloyd's of London. "I bear disquieting tidings," he announces gloomily. He introduces the inspector, who informs the group that Scotland Yard has incontrovertible proof that the man who robbed the Bank of England and Phileas Fogg are one and the same.

"Balderdash!" one responds. The others are equally disdainful. "A member of the Reform Club!" one exclaims. "My mind rejects the whole idea."

The inspector reveals further information: that morning the trading ship *Henrietta* departed New York with a cargo of cotton, lin-

seed oil, lumber—and Mr. Fogg and party—destination, Caracas, Venezuela. "We have no extradition treaty with Venezuela," he adds. "In other words, Mr. Fogg has bolted."

That moment, Mr. Fogg, on the bridge of a three-masted, paddle-wheeled sailing vessel, the *Henrietta*, hands over a large bundle of banknotes to the captain (Jack Oakie). The latter promptly orders his bewildered first mate (Andy Devine) to change course and proceed *east* by north, full speed ahead.

Later, the engineer (Edmund Lowe) turns to the helmsman as the vessel's long stack gives a final puff of smoke and the paddlewheels stop turning. "Well, there it is. The last spoonful of coal dust in the old scow."

Fogg, ever equal to any emergency, purchases the ship for the remaining sheaf of banknotes in his red carpetbag and, as the new owner, issues his first order: anything that will burn is to be piled into the stokehole. "The cargo first, of course," he says. "Then the upper decks, ladders, chairs, tables, bunks, everything—even the lifeboats. Is that clear?"

It is clear. The ship is literally chopped to pieces, ladders ripped from their frames, teak decking pried loose. The silhouette of the ship changes as the housings are torn away. Even Henrietta, the ship's bosomy figurehead, is fed to the flames.

But they are insufficient. The wheels slow down. Disconsolate, Mr. Fogg removes his silk hat, tosses it into the firebox and hurls his umbrella after it. All is lost...

"Land ho! Land ho!" the engineer shouts and, beyond the prow, emerges the faint outline of Britain.

Exultant, Fogg is about to board the London Express in Liverpool when Inspector Fix, armed with a warrant and flanked by two bobbies, arrests him in the Queen's name. "Thought you could outwit me, didn't you?" Fix chortles savagely.

Phileas Fogg sits in the loneliness of his gaol cell, so crushed he shows only a desultory interest in the solitary game of whist he is playing. It is 8:45 P.M., his deadline is up, his eighty days gone his wager and his fortune lost, irrevocably lost. Along with his proud name and reputation. Facing imprisonment as a common robber.

"The most shocking mistake…" Fogg looks up to see Inspector Fix, downcast and apologetic. "Never happened before in my career. The most terrible thing has happened, Mr. Fogg. The real culprit was apprehended in Brighton. I feel that I owe you a deep apology, sir…"

Fogg rises and faces Fix. "Now that you have successfully thwarted me and placed in my path the only obstacle I have been unable to predict, I feel that I can tell you I have never *really* enjoyed your company. Furthermore, you play an abominable game of whist. Good day, sir."

Princess Aouda and Passepartout await him outside his cell.

They return, a melancholy trio, to Fogg's house in London. The rooms are cheerless and dank. "Attend to the clocks," Fogg instructs Passepartout. "Get hold of Mr. MacMonnies and have them set in order. Right away…I mean tomorrow. Today's Sunday." Fogg starts upstairs, then is struck by an afterthought: "And turn off the gas in your room." It had been left burning eighty-one days ago.

That evening, Aouda brings Fogg a tea tray. She blames herself for the disaster. Had he not stopped to save her life in India, he would easily have won his wager. On the contrary, Fogg insists, he owes *her* an apology for bringing her to England, now that he is penniless.

She tries to comfort him. "In my country," she says, "it is said that misfortune, if shared with another sympathetic spirit, can be borne with resignation. Mr. Fogg, do you wish at once a kinswoman and a friend?" He stares at her puzzled. "Will you have me for your wife?" she asks.

There is a long pause. "Aouda—my darling!" He takes her in his arms.

A moment later, Fogg calls Passepartout on the speaking tube. "Arrange for a wedding," he says as if ordering breakfast.

"One wedding, sir. When?"

"Tomorrow, Monday."

"Olé! Olé!" Passepartout shouts joyously.

"Curtail the jubilation, if you please," says Fogg crisply. "And bring the Reverend Wilson."

On his return, with the Reverend Wilson in tow, Passepartout sees the sandwich-board of a news vendor, lettered SATURDAY'S RACE RESULTS!

Passepartout, almost past it, stops, turns and snatches the paper from the vendor. He stares at it, unable to believe his eyes. It is the *Morning Telegraph,* dated *Saturday,* September 21, 1872.

A Saturday paper hawked on Sunday? "Fiddlesticks!" snaps Fogg, upbraiding Passepartout for bolting into the room. "The printers must have made an error."

"It's Saturday! It's Saturday!" shrieks Passepartout. "We have ten minutes left!"

"We will review your impudence at a later date," says Fogg. "I have kept a complete record of every single phase of the trip. We went around the world in eighty days…this is the eighty-first day."

Passepartout continues to insist it is Saturday, not Sunday.

"We went eastward around the world, always moving toward the sun…" Fogg begins to recapitulate and suddenly stops. "Great heavens!" he exclaims. "We crossed the international dateline! We've gained an entire day. It *is* the twenty-first…this *is* the eightieth day." He takes out his two watches. "Eight thirty-four and ten seconds…we have ten minutes and fifty seconds left to get to the Club."

It is a nerve-shattering ordeal, the final ten minutes…

Fogg and Passepartout hop into a hansom cab whose driver (John Mills) is dozing. At last they shake him awake, but before he can go very far, he has an attack of hiccoughs that is contagious: in a moment the horse has started to hiccough. Fogg leaps down to continue afoot.

Dashing through the streets, his way is blocked by a mission band; a group of revivalists is gathered around its captain (Beatrice Lillie), who is exhorting the throng to fight the devil and refuse to be tempted down the paths of iniquity. *Continued on page 41*

Mike Todd at White Sands Guided
Missile Launching Site

Cantinflas on High-Wheeler
in London

The Wager Is Made
at Reform Club

Balloon Ascension in Paris

José Greco and His Flamenco Dancers in Spain

Bull Arena, Spain

Through the Indian Jungle

Bride Sacrificed on Suttee of Death

"Whist"-full Romance

Across Hong Kong on an Ostrich

Japanese Shrine

Pyrotechnics over San Francisco

Honky-Tonk Pianist

Dance Hall Hostess

Cantinflas at the Stake

Stripping of Henrietta

Bea Lillie's
Revivalists
Trap Niven

The Wager Is Won

Continued from page 32

Fogg is trapped and does not escape until he has tossed a fiver in the tambourine and sung a chorus from Hymn 579, "Have Courage, My Boy, to Say No!"

The Governor of the Bank of England and his associates who have taken Fogg's wager, wait in the card room of the Reform Club, licking their chops. The minute hand of the clock is moving between 8:44 and 8:45.

"Good heavens, why dither about like this?" says one impatiently. "He's lost the wager, twenty times over! Once he missed his trans-Atlantic connection…"

"No, no, chaps," the Governor stays them inflexibly. "Steady on, we're British gentlemen —play the game. Still fourteen seconds to go."

"The man isn't superhuman!" another comments.

"Phileas Fogg," the Governor says, "is the most punctual man alive."

"I trust I have not yet kept you waiting, gentlemen…"

They turn to see the precise Mr. Fogg as the minute hand of the clock touches 8:45, on time to the second.

As they give vent to a series of confused exclamations, Aouda suddenly appears in the doorway behind Fogg. There is an immediate, horrified hush.

"Great Ceasar's ghost!" exclaims the Governor. "A woman! In the *Club!*"

Fogg turns to his bride-to-be. "My dear, I must ask you to leave these precincts at once. No woman has ever set foot in the Club."

"But why not?" she asks, uncomprehending.

"Because that could spell the end of the British Empire." His expression of severity melts, and he takes her arm.

Suddenly there is a crash of windows being flung open and Passepartout, an ingratiating grin on his pixieish face, appears on the windowsill. Simultaneously a large painting on the wall crashes to the floor.

The Governor of the Bank of England voices the stupefaction of his fellow members. "This," he says lugubriously, "*is* the end."

THE production of *Around the World in 80 Days* made motion picture history, shattering records and precedents with Toddian profligacy. Among them:

The most stars ever to appear in a picture —fifty—each playing a role germane to the story and none appearing as himself.

The most people photographed in separate world-wide locations: 68,894 persons in thirteen different countries.

The most miles traveled to make a film: 4,000,000 air passenger miles.

The most sets ever used: 140 actual locations in addition to the stages of six major Hollywood studios, as well as studios in England, Hong Kong and Japan.

The most camera set-ups ever used: 2,000. (Gone with the Wind formerly held the record.)

The most costumes designed, made and/or rented: 74,685.

More species of animals photographed in their natural habitats.

The most properties employed in a film.

The most assistant directors: thirty-three.

The first time units of the Royal Thailand Navy are seen in a film.

The first time an elaborate full-length documentary (two hours' running time) was shot to record the behind-the-scenes shooting of the film.

To transport the film back and forth from locations to the laboratory at Fort Lee, New Jersey, where it was processed, required 1,500,000 air freight miles.

Airlines used on chartered flights included Air France, New Iberian, British European, Dutch KLM, Middle East, British Overseas A.C., Pakistan, Pan-American, Canadian Pacific Railway (which operates air service between Tokyo and Hong Kong), TWA, Japan Airlines, Frontier, Bonanza, American, Western, Braniff, Capitol, United, Southwest Airlines, California Central Airlines, Mercer Airlines, Paul Mantz and Aeronaves de Mexico.

More than 100,000 hot meals were served the cast and crew during shooting — including 8,972 bottles of wine supplied in Spain and France to wash down 26,391 location lunches; 4,220 pots of tea brewed for the extras during the London sequences; 3,660 doughnuts dunked in 2,869 gallons of coffee between meals on the various sets in Hollywood and 289 hot lunches dispensed ten miles out to sea during the shooting of the *Henrietta* sequence.

Thirty-four different species of animals were used in key scenes, a total of 7,959 in all, among them fifteen elephants, four trained ostriches, two deer, six trained

F I R S T WITH THE MOST

skunks, a sacred cow that would munch flowers on cue, 2,448 American buffalo, 3,800 Rocky Mountain sheep, the last remaining herd of Texas longhorn cattle, 17 fighting bulls, more than 800 horses, 12 Mongolian ponies, a dozen matched Palominos, 950 burros, a colt, 78 ducks, 48 geese, 97 hens, a dozen turkeys, 65 goats, four oxen, a dozen dogs and 512 Rhesus monkeys. One of the elephants, Big Babe, age sixty, stood nine feet three inches and weighed 8,700 pounds in his bare feet.

Ninety handlers, under the supervision of Kenny Lee, were required for the animals.

Thirteen cameras, including nine Todd-AO cameras, worth more than $600,000 were used, in addition to sound equipment valued at one million dollars.

More means of travel were employed than any other film. Not counting the 55 trucks, hundreds of thousands of miles of railroad transportation and 5,500,000 miles of air travel (passenger and freight) to make the picture, the script called for one or more principals (David Niven, Cantinflas, Robert Newton and/or Shirley MacLaine) to travel from:

CHELSEA TO VICTORIA SQUARE, LONDON — by BICYCLE

LONDON TO PARIS — by BOAT TRAIN

PARIS TO FIGUERAS, SPAIN — by BALLOON

SPAIN TO MARSEILLES — on SCHOONER

MARSEILLES TO SUEZ — on R.M.S. MONGOLIA

SUEZ TO BOMBAY — on R.M.S. MONGOLIA

BOMBAY TO KHOLBY — by GREAT INDIAN PENINSULA RAILWAY — ENGLISH INDIAN TRAIN

KHOLBY TO ALLAHABAD — by ELEPHANT

ALLAHABAD TO CALCUTTA — by GREAT INDIAN PENINSULA RAILWAY

CALCUTTA TO BANGKOK — on S.S. RANGOON — ROYAL BARGE

BANGKOK TO HONG KONG — on S.S. RANGOON

EAST HONG KONG TO WEST HONG KONG — by OSTRICH

HONG KONG TO YOKOHAMA — on CHINESE JUNK (RED SAILS)

YOKOHAMA TO JAPANESE CIRCUS — by RICKSHAW

YOKOHAMA TO SAN FRANCISCO — on S.S. GRANT

SAN FRANCISCO TO FT. KEARNEY — by AMERICAN PACIFIC RAILROAD

FT. KEARNEY TO MEDICINE BOW — by SADDLE HORSE AND STAGE COACH

MEDICINE BOW TO OMAHA — by SAILMOBILE

NEW YORK TO LIVERPOOL — on S.S. HENRIETTA

LIVERPOOL TO LONDON — by TRAIN

SAYVILLE ROW TO REFORM CLUB — by HANSOM CAB

It is the first motion picture made by the great Cantinflas outside of Latin America, the first motion picture directed by Michael Anderson in the United States, and the first motion picture produced anywhere by Michael Todd.

43

From Flashes to Smashe

by BILL DOLL

(The writer has, for twenty years, been Minister of Propaganda for Michael Todd's Theatrical Empire. Here for the first time, he ruffles the drum for Michael Todd, Jr.)

IN 1939 I wrote a short biographical sketch for the souvenir program of *The Hot Mikado*. I called it "From Flashes to Smashes with Michael Todd," basing the first part of the title upon the explosive effect achieved when the costume burned from the shapely body of the Flame Dancer.

It was the Flame Dance, a carnival act originated and presented by Todd, that served to catapult him toward a career in show business where one surprising smash has followed another throughout the years.

"From Flashes to Smashes with Michael Todd" has appeared as the frontispiece in Todd programs from that day to this, growing longer with each successive show by the cheap, and laggardly, journalistic device of simply updating the final paragraph.

Hawked in theater lobbies, in stadia, in arenas, from coast to coast, wherever a Todd show has played, the sale of "Flashes to Smashes" has gone well over the ten-million mark — outdistancing, at least numerically — even *Gone with the Wind*.

I have an affection for this old story, for I grew up with it, although now, reluctantly, I know that it will have to go. There's a new

signature on my paycheck these days, and where before there was only one Todd, now there are two. The time has come to sound the tocsin for Michael Todd, Jr.

Readying a return to the Broadway that he forsook to foment the celluloid tempest that changed the structure of the movie industry, Todd, the elder, flies his banner over Jules Verne's classic global saga, *Around the World in Eighty Days*. This show on film boasts the participation of half a hundred ranking stars, and utilizes the optical magic of Todd-AO which he, himself, developed.

Todd, the younger, will serve as General Manager of the Rivoli Theater where *Around the World* will be unreeled. Although this marks his first performance in a titular capacity, his working background in the Todd Tong is a lengthy one.

In 1940, at the age of eleven, he had a distinguished, not to say profitable, season as the employees' soda pop concessionaire of his Dad's sprawling amusement acreage at the New York World's Fair. From that time, until the date of his matriculation at Lawrenceville in 1944, it was almost impossible not to stumble over him backstage at one or another of the Old Man's Broadway attractions. I seem to recall that he was frequently to be seen doing his homework in Gypsy Rose Lee's dressing room throughout the run of *Star and Garter*.

At Lawrenceville, Junior is remembered as the most successful Prom Chairman in the entire history of the School. Entrusted with the few hundred dollars that had been subscribed, he was enjoined to engage the orchestra for the annual dance. Come Prom night, faculty and student body alike were nonplused to find Les Brown and his entire band on the podium.

The expensive musical aggregation, even then at a high point of fame, had responded without a quibble to Junior's sub-minimum offer. It seems that when Brown was a struggling band leader back in the early forties he was launched into the big brackets by Mike Senior who hired him to play at Michael Todd's Theater Café, that super Chicago saloon.

Sad to say, Junior was not on hand to accept the kudos for this stratagem, since—on the eve of his triumph—he was kicked in the head at football practice and sat out all the dances in the campus infirmary.

During adolescent summers, Junior pursued his theatrical bent by learning about stage lighting at a rural playhouse in Priscilla Beach, Mass.; serving as a part-time *Variety* mug, and stage managing Joan Blondell's barn tour of *Happy Birthday.*

He went through Amherst, majoring in English and philosophy, and graduated in 1952 after contriving a sabbatical interlude during which he worked his way around the world as a seaman on a freighter. He has just completed a three-year hitch in the Navy, emerging as a Lieutenant jg. On the day he was commissioned, he married Sarah Jane Weaver, the girl next door.

The Todds, Pére et Fils, first became a working team in the summer of 1950, when Pére Todd was supervising the production of the original Cinerama films. Junior was the unit manager of the crew shooting the Niagara Falls sequences.

For the record, Michael Junior can take credit for shooting the most talked-about scene in all of the new motion picture processes. This is the roller-coaster sequence in Cinerama. He went to Rockaway Beach with two technicians and a cameraman, promoted the use of the roller coaster, and shot the ride in a couple of hours. That the scene was so successful is the more incredible because it was shot with short ends of film, so that the action had to be picked up at the identical place on the runway after each strip had run through the camera.

Later he toured Europe with a five-man crew making footage in Edinburgh, and filming the Vienna Boys Choir. Those languorous shots of the canals of Venice in the first Cinerama were shot after Mike Senior had left town and cautioned him, "Don't waste film."

Of the roller-coaster film, Junior likes to point out that — exclusive of salaries — it cost just thirty-three dollars. This went for renting a station wagon and buying bolts to fasten the camera to the careening car.

He is not so proud of the fact that the following year, while his father was producing *A Night in Venice* at Jones Beach, he persuaded him to bring in the Cypress Garden Water Show as a daytime attraction. "It was a good show, but it just couldn't compete with the beach itself. It cost Dad $36,000."

Around early spring of 1956, Michael Todd, Jr., contributed an heir to the dynasty. Michael Todd became a grandfather. The baby was named Cyrus Clagett Todd.

In time to come when that name is to be arranged on theater marquee, or lobby frame, it is my reconciled intention to shuffle to one side and gracefully bequest this task to some future member of my shapeless profession. Two generations, they tell me, is par for the course.

45

The PLAYERS

DAVID NIVEN

as

Phileas Fogg

"**W**HAT do you think of the part of Phileas Fogg in *Around the World in Eighty Days?*" Mike Todd asked him.

"It's my favorite part in fiction," he said unhesitatingly. "I'd play it for nothing."

"You got a deal!" said Todd, grasping his hand.

"It took me several weeks to get a contract with money," says David Niven with a twinkling smile.

Phileas Fogg is described by Jules Verne, author of *Around the World in Eighty Days,* as a gentleman "of tall figure . . . with noble countenance, unwrinkled forehead, magnificent teeth" and a zealous interest in whist.

Niven, six-feet-four and 187 pounds, blue eyes and reddish hair, a graduate of Sandhurst, handsome, dignified and charming, elegantly fulfills Verne's conception of Fogg although his affection for whist is something less than passionate.

Born in Kirriemuir, Canada, the son of an Army captain, Niven began what he intended as a career with the Highland Light Infantry in Malta, returned to England for advanced military training, then lost interest in the military and resigned his commission. Adventure called . . .

To the lumber camps of Canada, to a London wine firm's office in New York, to gunnery officer for a band of revolutionists in Cuba, to a Japanese freighter bound for the Canal Zone, to Hollywood and a long-term contract with Samuel Goldwyn.

The "long-term" ended four years later, in 1939, the day England declared war on Germany. Niven left at once for England. He joined the Rifle Brigade as a second lieutenant, survived the disaster of Dunkirk, joined the Commandos, transferred to the top-secret Phantom Reconnaissance, wound up with the British Liberation Army in the invasion of France and was not demobilized until the surrender of Germany, after six years' active service, with the rank of Colonel.

Niven and his wife, Hjordis, a Swedish girl, live in Los Angeles with David, Jr., and Jamie, his sons by his first wife, who died in a tragic accident shortly after their return to this country following the war.

He starred in many notable films, among them the controversial and successful *The Moon is Blue,* but henceforth, indubitably, he will be identified with that quintessence of precision, Phileas Fogg.

CANTINFLAS

as

Passepartout

"CANTINFLAS is the world's greatest comedian," according to Charles Chaplin, who is not accustomed to making such statements twenty times a day.

Certainly he is the highest paid entertainer in the world, with a minimum income of $100,000 per *month,* mostly from the royalties of his films.

Also, he is the No. 1 philanthropist in show business. In 1952 he launched a social improvement program in Mexico and pledged to raise 20,000,000 pesos a year to build housing units, hospitals and clinics for the poor. The colony, called Madelena Michuca, now has sixty-four buildings.

He would have become, in the opinion of many great bullfighters, an outstanding matador if he had elected to follow the tradition of the Corrida instead of satirizing it. Since the death of the immortal Manolete, he is the only man who can consistently fill the world's largest bull ring, at Mexico City, with a capacity of 70,000.

There, for charity, as well as in *Around the World in 80 Days* (in which, *without doubles,* he engaged in a protracted and dangerous duel) he faces the bulls, at forty-one, with the scars of a terrible goring he received some years ago in Peru.

The poor literally pawn their shoes to see him. To discourage families from giving up their clothes and furniture to buy tickets, the government closes all pawnshops as a matter of policy two days before his appearances in the bull ring.

This is the man—born Mario Moreno, son of a postal employee; President of the Association of Mexican actors, the idol of Latin America for almost a quarter of a century, a legend in his time—who refused countless offers to appear in the United States.

Until he heard Mike Todd's siren song.

"A pleasant companion reduces the length of a journey," said Publilius Syrus in 50 B.C.

Cantinflas brings to life in Passepartout the perfect traveling companion. Behind him, as if in rehearsal for the part, are twenty years with a *carpa,* or traveling tent show, in which he learned to be a singer, dancer, acrobat, prize fighter and clown. From the *carpa* too came his wife, Valentina Zubareff, a dancer.

His stage name, which had no meaning when he conceived it, has become, because of his overwhelming popularity, a part of the Mexican language. As a verb, *cantinflear* means to talk much, say little and indulge in frenetic nonsequiturs, similar to his patter. As a noun, it means a lovable clown, the character he portrays.

Cantinflas, the most popular figure in the history of Latin American entertainment, now will undoubtedly take a place among the world's princes of comedy.

It will be simple.

Passepartout, as any French 1 student will tell you, means master-key.

SHIRLEY MACLAINE

as

Princess Aouda

IT IS typical of Mike Todd that, after attaining a constellation of fifty stars, more than forty-five for "bit" parts, he selected a twenty-two-year-old unknown as the leading lady of his multi-multi-million production.

Why Shirley MacLaine?

"She's believable, yet has that pixie quality," says Todd.

Mr. Todd notwithstanding, Shirley MacLaine is not believable—to Shirley MacLaine. At times, it seems like a dream, a dream that began in 1954, the third night of the Broadway musical comedy hit, *Pajama Game*.

Shortly before the performance, the star, Carol Haney, injured her ankle and could not go on. Shirley, her understudy, took her place.

Hal Wallis, the veteran motion picture producer, who had come from Hollywood to see Miss Haney, was so impressed by Miss MacLaine that he placed her under contract before he left the theater.

Her first film, on loan-out to Paramount, was in Alfred Hitchcock's *The Trouble with Harry*. Wallis then cast her in *Artists and Models* with Martin and Lewis. *Around the World in 80 Days* is her third picture.

Born in Richmond, Virginia, the daughter of a former Little Theater actress and a former band leader, she made her professional debut, at sixteen, as a dancer in the chorus of *Oklahoma!* Trained as a dancer since the age of three, she does not dance a step in this picture, naturally.

In 1955 she married Steve Parker, a young actor, who is now her business manager.

There is not a first-rate writer, director, producer or star in Hollywood who would buy the story of an obscure understudy who, given her chance when the star sprains her ankle, becomes the leading lady of one of the biggest and most expensive films in the history of motion pictures. It's too corny.

No one did buy it—except Mike Todd. Why?

"Life is corny," says he.

ROBERT NEWTON

as

Inspector Fix

"**B**OB NEWTON was born to play Inspector Fix," remarked David Niven who, as Phileas Fogg, is shadowed by him in his frenetic chase around the world.

One month after he finished the picture, Newton died, of a heart attack, in the arms of his wife, Vera Budnick.

His Inspector Fix is the last—and perhaps the greatest—in a gallery of memorable portraits etched by a master.

They'll remember Bob Newton . . .

They'll remember his Pistol in Sir Laurence Olivier's *Henry V*.

They'll remember his classic villainy in *Jamaica Inn* and *Odd Man Out, The Beachcomber* and *Androcles and the Lion, Major Barbara* and *Gaslight,* his Bill Sykes in *Oliver Twist* and his John Silver in *Treasure Island*.

They'll remember his inimitable rich voice, his wink, his leer, his roaring laugh.

He was a nonconformist, his own man on and off the stage.

He worked hard and played hard, he drank hard and loved hard.

He was an Artist. Upper-case. His mother was a writer, his father, sister and brother were painters.

He was an Actor. Upper-case, in the finest tradition of the English stage, from his professional debut at the age of fifteen with the British Repertory Company—through his apprenticeship as an actor and stage manager with a touring company in Canada, South Africa, Australia and the West Indies—to Broadway, replacing Laurence Olivier in Noel Coward's *Private Lives*—to his great years and, at last, his final scene as Inspector Fix.

He was a gifted man, sensitive, warm-hearted, rebellious.

Being original, he was an enemy of convention.

Being an Artist, he despised mediocrity.

His like will not come this way again.

CAMEOS

CHARLES BOYER (M. Gasse, Clerk, Thomas Cook, Paris). Born in Figeac just before the turn of the century, Charles Boyer was educated in Paris at the Sorbonne and the Paris Conservatory. He made his stage debut in 1920 in *Jardin des Murcie* and for the next fifteen years his professional activities alternated between the French stage and screen. His Paris plays include *L'Homme Enchaîné* and *Galerie des Glaces Melo*.

In 1935 Mr. Boyer went to Hollywood where he quickly became one of the most popular leading men. Among his more memorable pictures are *Mayerling, Back Street, Love Affair, Algiers, Hold Back the Dawn, Arch of Triumph,* and *The Earrings of Madame de—*.

He made his Broadway bow in 1948 in *Red Gloves*, has since appeared with the First Drama Quartet in *Don Juan in Hell* and in *Kind Sir*. Boyer has also been seen in many television programs.

JOE E. BROWN (Station Master, Fort Kearney). A native of Helgate, Ohio, born in 1892, Brown ran away to join the circus at the age of nine. After playing professional baseball for several seasons, he entered show business in earnest, touring in *Listen, Lester,* then in vaudeville and later starring on Broadway in such productions as *Greenwich Village Follies, Betsy Lee* and *Captain Jinks*.

Brown went to Hollywood in 1928 and has been making pictures ever since. For three years he was one of the top ten box-office stars. His movies include *Burlesque, On with the Show, Hold Everything, Elmer the Great, A Midsummer Night's Dream, The Daring Young Man* and *Showboat*.

Some years ago he returned to the stage to play *Harvey*. In 1953 Brown was tapped for TV's "This Is Your Life" program.

MARTINE CAROL (Girl in Railroad Station, Paris). The epitome of French femininity, Mlle. Carol was born Maryse Maurer in Biarritz in 1924. She attended schools at Pau and Neuilly-sur-seine, studied piano and painting. In 1941 she made her stage debut in Paris.

Two years later her phenomenally successful cinema career began with *La Ferme aux Loups*. Since then she has appeared in some thirty films. She quickly became the highest paid actress in France. In recent years she has starred in *Wedding Night, Love and*

Desire, Lucrezia Borgia, Adorable Creatures, Darling Caroline's Caprice, Madame du Barry, Nana, Lola, and *The Diary of Major Thompson*.

In 1946 Mlle. Carol appeared on the stage in a French production of *Tobacco Road*.

JOHN CARRADINE (Colonel Proctor, San Francisco Politico). A native New Yorker, John Carradine was educated at the Episcopal Academy and Graphic Art School in Philadelphia, Pennsylvania, and at the New York Art School.

His dramatic career began at the age of nineteen in *Camille* at the St. Charles Theater, New Orleans, in 1925. Mr. Carradine then became a marine artist and portrait painter and subsequently a designer for Cecil B. de Mille.

In 1928 he launched his career in Hollywood, and subsequently appeared in the widest span of pictures, from Westerns like *Stagecoach* to musicals like *Alexander's Ragtime Band* and spectacles like *The Ten Commandments*.

Carradine returned to the stage in 1941. He toured with his own Shakespearean repertory company, and in 1946 made his first appearance on Broadway in *The Duchess of Malfi*. His other New York roles included Voltore in *Volpone*, Nyunin in *The Wedding* and the Ragpicker in *The Madwoman of Chaillot*.

CHARLES COBURN (Clerk, Hong Kong Steamship Office). Though born in Savannah, Georgia, in 1877, Charles Coburn more often than not has been mistaken for an Englishman. He attributes this to the fact that he received his training in Shakespearean drama and that he made his biggest hit on Broadway playing a British tommy in *The Better 'Ole* for two years during and after World War I.

He began his career as a program boy at the Savannah Theater at the age of fourteen. He first appeared on the New York stage at the Fourteenth Street Theatre in 1901 in *Up York State*. Several years later he organized the Coburn Shakespearean Players, which he and his wife, actress Ivah Wills, maintained for many years.

Mr. Coburn moved to Hollywood in 1938. Since then he has contributed many notable cinema characterizations, especially his role in *The More the Merrier* for which, in 1943, he won the Academy Award as the best supporting actor.

In 1946 he reappeared on the stage, touring for the Theatre Guild as Sir John Falstaff in *The Merry Wives of Windsor*. He has supervised the annual Mohawk Drama

Festival at Union College, Schenectady, New York, since its inauguration in 1934 and received the honorary degree of Master of Letters from the college for this work.

RONALD COLMAN (Official of Great Indian Peninsular Railway). Born in Richmond, Surrey, Ronald Colman was a well-known amateur actor by the age of seventeen. He made his professional debut in 1914 a few months before the start of World War I. At the outbreak of war he went to France with the London Scottish Regiment.
He was invalided out of the service in 1916, and in the same year appeared on the London stage in *The Maharani of Arakan.*

After a number of hits in London, he toured the U. S. in *The Dauntless Three* and with Fay Bainter in *East Is West.* His first appearance on Broadway was in 1921 as the Temple Priest in *The Green Goddess*, with George Arliss. He soon became a matinée idol and, while appearing in *La Tendresse* in 1923, he was signed as leading man opposite Lillian Gish in the motion picture *The White Sister.*

Mr. Colman was an immediate success in Hollywood and has not returned to the stage. Among his notable successes are *The Prisoner of Zenda, Bulldog Drummond, Raffles, Arrowsmith, A Tale of Two Cities* and *Lost Horizon.* In 1947 he won the Academy Award as the best actor for his performance in *A Double Life.*

In recent years Mr. Colman has appeared on TV with his wife, actress Benita Hume, in a series "The Halls of Ivy."

MELVILLE COOPER (Steward, R.M.S. Mongolia). A veteran of British repertory, G. Melville Cooper was born in Birmingham, England, in 1896. His theatrical career, begun in 1914 at Stratford-on-Avon, was postponed five years by the first world war. On his return from the Army, he joined the Birmingham Repertory Company and played many important roles in every manner of play.

He made his first London appearance in 1924 in *The Tragedy of an Elderly Gentleman (Back to Methuselah).* His greatest London success was as Trotter in *Journey's End.* After playing the King in *Jubilee* he went to California and made a number of movies, notably *The Scarlet Pimpernel, 13 Rue Madeleine* and *Father of the Bride.*

Since 1943 he has spent most of his time on the New York stage, returning once to London to appear in *Romany Love.* His most recent Broadway plays were *The Day After Tomorrow, Make a Wish* and *Escapade.*

NOEL COWARD (Roland Hesketh-Baggott, Manager of London Employment Agency). If any contemporary artist has become a true legend in his time, Noel Coward most certainly has: as an actor, director, producer, author and composer in every medium of communication and entertainment.
Born in 1899 at Teddington, England, he made his theatrical debut as Prince Mussel in a children's play, *The Goldfish,* in 1911. Among other early parts Coward played were Slightly in *Peter Pan* and Charley in

Charley's Aunt. In 1917 he joined the Army and returned to the theater in December, 1918, in *Scandal.*

The first of his forty-some plays and revues, *I'll Leave It to You,* was produced in 1920. In 1925 he made his New York debut in his play *The Vortex.* For some years thereafter he alternated between England and the United States. The best known of his works in which he appeared on Broadway are *This Year of Grace, Private Lives, Design for Living* (with the Lunts) and *Tonight at 8:30.*

Other well-known Coward plays in which the author has appeared are *Conversation Piece, Present Laughter, This Happy Breed* and *Blithe Spirit,* which ran in London for 1,997 performances, the longest run on record for a non-musical play. In 1948 he played a role in the French version—*Joyeux Chagrins*—of *Present Laughter.*

Mr. Coward first appeared in motion pictures in 1917 in *Hearts of the World,* directed by D. W. Griffith. In 1934 he made *The Scoundrel* in New York.

He is the author of six volumes, *A Withered Nosegay, Terribly Intimate Portraits, Poems of Hermina Whittlebot, Post Mortem, Sketches and Lyrics* and *Spangled Unicorn;* his autobiography, *Present Indicative,* was published in 1937, his first novel in 1939 and *Middle East Diary* in 1945.

FINLAY CURRIE (Member of the Reform Club, London). Long a stand-by of the British stage and screen, Finlay Currie was born in 1878 in Edinburgh, Scotland. There he made his first stage appearance and subsequently engaged in concert work, for a time appeared with Adeler and Sutton's Pierrots.

His London debut was made under the name of Harry Calvo, the double-voiced vocalist, in 1902. He toured England, then did a monologue in New York at Tony Pastor's. He spent ten years touring Australia as principal comedian in Sir Benjamin Fuller's company.

Returning to London in 1930, Mr. Currie appeared alternately in plays and movies. Among his stage hits were *The Last Mile, The Skipper Next to God* and *Death of a Salesman.*

His outstanding pictures include *Great Expectations, Treasure Island* and *Trio.*

REGINALD DENNY (Inspector, Bombay Police). Reginald Denny made his initial stage appearance in London at the age of seven. Two years later he portrayed Peter in *Scrooge* in the first Command Performance given before King Edward VII.
Born in Richmond, Surrey, in 1891, Denny attended St. Xavier's College in Sussex. After graduation he toured the world in comic operas. His first of many appearances in this country was in *The Quaker Girl* in 1911. He served with the Royal Flying Corps from 1917 to 1919, then returned to America and acted in straight plays.

His movie career began in England in 1914. His first hit was *The Leather Pushers.* Mr. Denny has made many American pictures, including *The Macomber Affair, Rebecca* and *The Lost Patrol.*

In addition to his career in the entertainment world, Denny pioneered and developed the first pilotless radio-controlled aircraft sucessfully flown in the U. S. He was Vice-President and Secretary of the Radioplane Company, 1940-9, formed to carry out research and build radio-controlled target planes for the U. S. Armed Forces. The U. S. Navy prototype plane initials T.D.D. stand for *Target Drone Denny.*

 **ANDY DEVINE (First Mate, S. S. Henrietta).** Born in Flagstaff, Arizona, in 1905, Devine graduated from Santa Clara University. He started in films in 1926 as an extra. After appearing in a series of collegiate shorts, where his talents as a "fall guy" were thoroughly exploited, he graduated into features. He has played in such films as *All Quiet on the Western Front, The Spirit of Notre Dame, All American, Ali Baba and the Forty Thieves, Follow the Boys* and *The Red Badge of Courage.*

In recent years, Devine has concentrated his efforts almost exclusively on Westerns. He has appeared on TV in the "Wild Bill Hickok" and "Andy's Gang" shows.

 **MARLENE DIETRICH (Owner, Barbary Coast Saloon).** Marlene Dietrich was born in Berlin in December, 1904. The daughter of a noble but impoverished Prussian officer, she was christened Maria Magdalene von Losch. Educated at private schools, Weimar University and the Berlin Musical Academy, Miss Dietrich intended to become a violinist. A severe wrist injury put an end to that ambition. She then studied at Max Reinhardt's School of the Drama, and made her stage debut in Vienna in a German-language production of *Broadway.*

Subsequently, she appeared in a number of Reinhardt's productions in Berlin. There she met and married Rudolf Sieber, the stage manager of the UFA motion picture studios. Their daughter, Maria (now Maria Riva, well-known stage and TV actress), was born in 1926.

Four years later, Josef von Sternberg picked Miss Dietrich for her first film role in *The Blue Angel,* which made her an international celebrity. In the United States she repeated her sensational success in such movies as *Morocco, Dishonored, Shanghai Express, Scarlet Empress, Song of Songs, Kismet, Destry Rides Again* and *Golden Earrings.*

During World War II, she gave up Hollywood completely for three years in order to entertain the troops. Serving in the U.S.O., she traveled constantly, from the Aleutians to the Anzio beachhead. She gave four shows a day, visited hospitals, once stood for six hours in the bitter cold of dawn waving her arms to flights of paratroopers. She caught pneumonia, was under fire several times and was nearly captured by the Nazis, who threatened to shoot her if they caught her. For her untiring, unglamorous work and exposure to danger near the front lines, she was awarded the medal of the Legion of Honor by France and the Medal of Freedom by the United States.

Miss Dietrich in recent years has had her own radio programs, made several extremely popular record albums and been paid fabulous sums for supper club appearances on the Continent, in England and the U. S. A.

Her sympathy and generosity are legendary. After the war she clothed the entire staff of a French studio. At the time that she was decorated for her war service, the American Veterans' Committee noted: "Her own courage under fire inspired those of us who sometimes grew doubtful—her smile never failed to force one from our own tired souls—her songs always reminded us that the world might sing again."

 **LUIS MIGUEL DOMINGÚIN (Bullfighter, Spain).** One of Spain's most famous matadors, Luis Miguel Domingúin appears in and staged the bullfight sequences of the picture.

A prodigy of the arena, Domingúin started fighting professionally at the age of twelve. He was born in Seville in 1922 and practiced bullfighting in the same way American boys play baseball. After gaining experience in the smaller rings, he made his debut in Madrid in 1941 and in a few years had reached the top.

Son and brother of matadors, Domingúin owns many of Spain's bull rings. He retired from bullfighting in 1953, at the peak of his career, to take up the life of a rancher. He has a home in Salicas Cuenca, seventy miles from Chinchon, where the movie's bullfight scenes were staged, and breeds bulls for rings throughout the Latin world. Soon after his movie debut in *Around the World in 80 Days,* Domingúin made a sensationally successful return to the ring in South America.

 **FERNANDEL (Coachman, Paris).** Fernandel is, in the opinion of *Life* magazine, "France's greatest comic attraction."

Born Fernand Joseph Désiré Contandin in Marseilles in 1903, Fernandel started in show business at the age of five in a melodrama at the Theatre Chave. He has appeared in more than 110 motion pictures since 1930. In 1937 he made *Angèle,* his first movie under Marcel Pagnol's direction.

Fernandel is best known in this country for his tragicomic roles in *The Well-Digger's Daughter* and *The Little World of Don Camillo. The Red Inn, The French Touch* and *The Sheep Has Five Legs* have also been well received in the U. S. A.

In 1949, photographer Philippe Halsman published *The Frenchman,* a book which contains twenty-four pictures of the actor's incomparable Gallic physiognomy as he answered questions in pantomime. The book sold more than 100,000 copies.

He is a Chevalier of the Legion of Honor and an officer of the French Academy, and has been awarded the *Palmes Académiques.* He collects rare editions of Molière.

 **SIR JOHN GIELGUD (Foster, Fogg's Ex-Valet).** One of the foremost Shakespearean actors in the world, Sir John Gielgud has played Hamlet more than five hundred times. He is also a producer and director of note and in 1953 was knighted for his services to the British stage.

Born in London in 1904, Sir John went to Westminster School, then studied for the stage at Lady

Benson's school and the Royal Academy of Dramatic Art. His professional debut was made at the age of seventeen in *Henry V* at the Old Vic. Gielgud made his first New York appearance in *The Patriot* in 1928.

He rejoined the Old Vic Company in 1929. His 1935 production of *Romeo and Juliet,* in which he played Romeo, achieved the longest run on record for this play. The following year he produced and played *Hamlet* in New York and London; again his production achieved the longest run on record for the play.

Gielgud has appeared in a number of movies, beginning with *Insult* and *The Good Companions* in 1932. He played Disraeli in *The Prime Minister* in 1940. His most recent picture is *Richard III.*

In 1950 he received the honorary degree of Doctor of Laws of St. Andrews University. He published his autobiography, *Early Stages,* in 1939.

HERMIONE GINGOLD (Tart, London). Born in London near the turn of the century, Miss Gingold studied for the theater under Rosina Filippi and made her debut in 1908 as the Herald in *Pinkie and the Fairies.* A long and successful career in Shakespearean and other dramas followed. In the 1930's she added singing to her other accomplishments, and has since then appeared in a number of London revues, including *The Gate Revue* and *Swinging the Gate.* From 1943 through 1948 she played in three revues, entitled *Sweet and Low, Sweeter and Lower,* and *Sweetest and Lowest.*

Several seasons ago Miss Gingold made her Broadway debut in John Murray Anderson's *Almanac.* She has appeared in numerous British films. *Around the World in 80 Days* is her first American picture, but it wasn't necessary for her to leave London to play the part.

JOSÉ GRECO (Dancer, Cave of the Seven Winds). One of the foremost exponents of the Spanish dance, José Greco was born forty-one years ago of Spanish and Italian parentage in Montorio nei Frentani, a village in the Abruzzi mountains of Italy. He spent three impressionable years in Seville absorbing the traditional flamenco dances before coming to America at the age of ten. Greco left high school at fourteen to study painting, but after seeing the famous Spanish dancer, Vicente Escudero, he decided to concentrate on dancing. Greco had been studying for two years when he was noticed in rehearsal by the ballet mistress of the old New York Hipprodome Opera Company. She gave him a job in *Carmen.*

In 1942 he joined La Argentinita's ensemble of flamenco dancers. After her death he danced with his sister, Pilar López. Invited in 1948 to do the choreography for a dance sequence in a bullfight film, *Manolete,* he organized a troupe of dancers to perform the work. The success of this ballet encouraged him to form his own company which, since 1951, has made four record-breaking tours of Europe and America. It is this company which is seen with him in *Around the World in 80 Days.*

SIR CEDRIC HARDWICKE (Sir Francis Cromarty, Bombay-Calcutta Train). Distinguished veteran of hundreds of plays, both classic and contemporary, Sir Cedric is also a producer of note and was knighted by George V in the New Year's Honors, 1934.

Born in Stourbridge, Worcestershire, in 1893, Hardwicke attended Bridgnorth School in Salop before enrolling in the Royal Academy of Dramatic Art. He made his stage debut in *The Monk and the Woman* in 1912 and then toured the provinces, South Africa and Rhodesia. After appearances in supporting roles at the Old Vic, he entered the army and served in France from 1914-21.

Following his war service, he was with the Birmingham Repertory Company for several years. In 1935 he made his first appearance on the New York stage, in *Promise.* Hardwicke returned to the U. S. three years later in *Shadow and Substance,* and after touring in this play, went to Hollywood where he remained until 1944.

Since, he has alternated between the British and American stage and cinema, appearing in some notable theater revivals including *Pygmalion, Antigone* and his own production of *Caesar and Cleopatra.* He was a member of the First Drama Quartet which toured the United States in Shaw's *Don Juan in Hell.*

Sir Cedric has appeared in numerous distinguished pictures in the U. S. A. and England, notably *Becky Sharp, The Winslow Boy, On Borrowed Time* and, most recently, *Richard III.*

In 1932 he issued a book of recollections, *Let's Pretend,* and in 1935 was elected Rede Lecturer to Cambridge University for the following year.

TREVOR HOWARD (Fallentin, Member of Reform Club). Born in Cliftonville, Kent, in 1916, Mr. Howard went to Clifton College and studied for the stage at the Royal Academy. He made his first appearance on the stage in *Revolt in a Reformatory.* He won the B. B. C. prize in 1934. After two years in London plays, he spent a season at the Memorial Theatre, Stratford-on-Avon. Howard became a matinée idol during the two-year London run of *French without Tears,* 1936-38. He returned to Stratford for another season, followed by two years of repertory at Colchester and Harrogate.

After being mustered out of the service in World War II, Howard made his cinema debut in *The Way Ahead.* He has appeared in such fine British pictures as *Brief Encounter, Outcast of the Islands, The Third Man* and *Odette.* He was one of the top ten box-office stars in Britain in the years 1948, 1951 and 1952.

GLYNIS JOHNS (Tart, London). Miss Johns was born in 1923 in Pretoria, South Africa. Her father was a prominent actor and her mother a pianist. Educated in England, she made her stage debut in London at the age of twelve in *Buckie's Bears.* After playing a number of juvenile roles, she starred in *A Kiss for Cinderella, Peter Pan* and *I'll See You Again.*

Equally popular on the screen, where she first appeared

in 1937, Miss Johns' pictures include *The Beachcomber, The Great Manhunt, No Highway in the Sky* and, most recently, the American movie *The Court Jester.*

She was voted one of the top ten box-office stars in Great Britain, 1951 to 1954.

BUSTER KEATON (Train Conductor, San Francisco to Fort Kearney). Born in Pickway, Kansas, 1896, Keaton started out in show business as a baby in a vaudeville sketch with his parents. He grew up with the circuits and, one of the first to recognize the future of films, moved to Hollywood after World War I to play in a series of comedies with Fatty Arbuckle.

Soon he struck out for himself and starred in a number of his own productions, gaining international fame as the poignant and hilarious "frozen-faced comedian." Some of his films, such as *The Navigator* and *The General,* are still considered among the funniest pictures ever made and established him as one of the great comics of our time.

Since the advent of talking pictures, he has appeared in many features, among them *That's the Spirit, You're My Everything, Limelight* and *Sunset Boulevard.*

A movie based on his life is being produced at Paramount.

EVELYN KEYES (Tart, Paris). Born in Port Arthur, Texas, in the mid-1920's, Miss Keyes made her professional debut as a dancer in night clubs. Her beauty and grace won her a film contract in Hollywood where she quickly established herself as a dramatic actress of considerable ability.

Her early motion pictures include *The Buccaneer, Union Pacific* and *Gone with the Wind.* Among her later movies are *A Thousand and One Nights, The Jolson Story, Mating of Millie, Johnny O'Clock, Enchantment, Mr. Soft Touch, The Prowler, The Killer That Stalked New York, Smuggler's Island, The Iron Man* and *Hell's Half Acre.*

BEATRICE LILLIE (Leader of Revivalist Group, London). The inimitable "Bea" Lillie was born in Toronto, Canada, just before the turn of the century. She attended St. Agnes' College in Ontario before making her way to London to pursue a stage career. Her London debut was made at the age of fifteen in *The Darling of Diane,* and for the next nine years she alternated between revues and straight comedies.

Her first New York appearance was with *André Charlot's Revue of 1924.* She followed that success with a dozen other musical hits on both sides of the Atlantic, notably *The Third Little Show, Walk a Little Faster, At Home Abroad, Tonight at 8:30, Seven Lively Arts* and *Inside U. S. A.* Her most recent appearance on Broadway, *An Evening with Beatrice Lillie,* was a huge success.

Since 1926, when she made *Exit Smiling,* Miss Lillie has appeared infrequently in motion pictures. Her best-known movie is *On Approval,* which Lillie fans in this country rush to see every time it is re-released.

She has frequently broadcast and appeared on television in the U. S. A. and in England, and has several times performed at the London night club, Café de Paris. During the war she traveled extensively to entertain the troops.

In private life Miss Lillie is Lady Peel, widow of Sir Robert Peel.

PETER LORRE (Japanese Steward, S. S. Carnatic). Peter Lorre was born in Rosenberg, Hungary, in 1904 and educated in Vienna. He ran away from home at the age of seventeen to join an improvised theater company and worked as a bank clerk while playing bit parts. He later appeared with the Galsworthy Society of Zurich, then acted in Vienna and Berlin.

In 1931 he received international acclaim for his unforgettable portrayal of the psychopathic murderer in Fritz Lang's motion picture, *M.* After movies made in France and England, he came to Hollywood in 1936. Among his most notable performances were those in *The Maltese Falcon, Mask of Dimitrios, Arsenic and Old Lace, Beat the Devil* and the Jules Verne epic *20,000 Leagues under the Sea.*

EDMUND LOWE (Chief Engineer, S. S. Henrietta). A native of San José, California, Lowe was born in 1892. Following his graduation from Santa Clara University, he started out in show business as a member of a Los Angeles stock company. After playing the lead in scores of plays, including *Roads to Destiny, The Son-Daughter* and *The Walk-Off,* he switched to motion pictures in 1923 and quickly became one of the box-office greats of the silent days.

Mr. Lowe's career successfully weathered the advent of the talkies. He has played in scores of memorable films, the most notable being *What Price Glory* and its successor, *The Cockeyed World.*

A. E. MATTHEWS, (Billiard Player, Reform Club). The dean of the London stage was born in Bridlington, Yorkshire, in 1869. His father was one of the Matthews Brothers of the original Christy Minstrels and his great-uncle was the famous clown, Tom Matthews.

Mr. Matthews began his long and distinguished career as a call boy in 1886 at the Princess Theatre in London. Within a few months he had advanced to assistant stage-manager of *Held by the Enemy,* in which, at one time or another, he played every male part except one.

In 1889 he toured South Africa, playing forty-three parts in twelve months, and later spent three years in Australia, in *Charley's Aunt* and *The Private Secretary.* New York audiences saw him first in 1910 in *Love Amongst the Lions.* Since then he has repeatedly journeyed to the U. S. A. to appear in some twenty plays on Broadway. London has seen him in more than sixty plays.

Mr. Matthews received the Order of the British Empire in the King's Birthday Honors, 1951.

MIKE MAZURKI (Drunk, Hong Kong Dive).
Born in Tarnopal, Austria, in 1909, Mazurki was educated in the United States, receiving his B.A. from Manhattan College in 1930. Big, tough and athletic, he played professional football for several seasons and got an indirect taste of show business as a wrestler.

In 1941, while appearing on the Los Angeles mat, he took time off to play in *The Shanghai Gesture*. Abandoning his wrestling career, he became a full-time actor, and has since been seen in such pictures as *Unconquered*, *Come to the Stable*, *Samson and Delilah*, *The Egyptian* and *Blood Alley*.

TIM McCOY (Commander of U. S. Cavalry, Fort Kearney). To play the role of a dashing U. S. Cavalry Colonel, Mr. Todd picked a real-life Colonel who is also a veteran of a dozen film campaigns against the Sioux, Tim McCoy.

Born in 1891 in Saginaw, Michigan, McCoy was educated at St. Ignatius College in Chicago. A crack horseback rider, he served for years in the United States Cavalry. During this period he became an authority on Indians.

A contract to make Western pictures followed, and he appeared for years in a series of action films, including *The Fighting Fool*, *Sioux Blood*, *Man of Action*, *Down Texas Way* and *Riders of the West*.

VICTOR McLAGLEN (Helmsman, S. S. Henrietta). Born in 1886 in London, McLaglen grew up in South Africa where his father was Bishop of Clermont. After serving in World War I, he became a professional boxer but soon switched to the relatively safe business of acting. He made his stage debut in London in *The Glorious Adventure* with Lady Diana Manners. After winning a reputation in the theater, both in the United States and abroad, he entered motion pictures. Among other films, he appeared in *What Price Glory*, *Beau Geste*, *The Cockeyed World*, *The Lost Patrol* and *The Quiet Man*.

In 1935, McLaglen won the Academy Award for best actor for his performance in *The Informer*.

JOHN MILLS (London Cabby). Born in 1908 in Suffolk, England, Mills tried business briefly before turning to the theater. His first stage appearance was in the chorus of *The Five O'Clock Girl* in London in 1929. Then he toured India as Lieut. Raleigh in *Journey's End* and in other vehicles. Returning to London, he played in musicals and straight plays, notably *Charley's Aunt*, *Cavalcade*, *A Midsummer Night's Dream*, *She Stoops to Conquer* and *Of Mice and Men*.

In 1932 Mr. Mills commenced his movie career and has appeared in such distinguished pictures as *Good-bye Mr. Chips*, *In Which We Serve*, *This Happy Breed*, *Great Expectations* and *Operation Disaster*.

He was one of the top British money-making stars in the cinema industry in 1945, 1946, 1947, 1949, 1950 and 1954.

ROBERT MORLEY (Ralph, a Governor of the Bank of England). Actor-playwright Robert Morley was originally intended for a diplomatic career. Born in Semley, Wiltshire, in 1908, he was educated at Wellington College and in Germany, France and Italy. But he decided his preference lay with the theater, and went off to London to study at the Royal Academy of Dramatic Art.

He made his stage debut at Margate in *Dr. Syn* when he was twenty. After a brief appearance in London as a pirate in *Treasure Island*, he toured with several plays and repertory companies. In 1935, in conjunction with Peter Bull, he established a repertory at Perranporth, Cornwall, where he played a number of parts. The following year, in the title role of *Oscar Wilde*, he scored a personal success which was repeated two years later on Broadway. In between he scored again as Alexandre Dumas in *The Great Romancer*. Several years later Morley triumphed as Sheridan Whiteside in *The Man Who Came to Dinner*, remaining in this play for nearly three years.

In 1947 he appeared in *Edward, My Son*, which he co-authored with Noel Langley. He took the play to New York and later to Australia and New Zealand. His most recent performances were in *The Little Hut* and *Hippo Dancing*.

In addition to *Edward, My Son* and *Hippo Dancing*, Mr. Morley has written several other plays—*Short Story*, *Goodness, How Sad*, *Staff Dance* and *The Full Treatment* (with Ronald Gow).

He entered pictures in 1937 and has appeared in *Marie Antoinette*, *Major Barbara*, *Young Mr. Pitt*, *The African Queen* and *Beau Brummell*.

EDWARD R. MURROW, Prologue Commentator. "My father, a farmer," Mr. Murrow relates, "does not go so far as to say that there's something dishonest about a man's making a living merely by talking. But he does think there's something doubtful about it."

The "talking" Mr. Murrow was born in Greensboro, North Carolina, in 1908. His family soon afterward moved to the state of Washington, and Edward went to school there. In 1930 he graduated from Washington State College, where he majored in history and speech and was a Phi Beta Kappa.

After graduation, as president of the National Student Federation, he traveled extensively in America and Europe. In 1932 he was appointed assistant director of the Institute of International Education in charge of foreign offices. With the I. I. E., "eight of us set up an emergency committee. We raised a million and a half dollars and brought out ninety of the best minds from Nazi Germany. It was the most satisfying thing I ever did."

Mr. Murrow's first post at CBS was Director of Talks and Education. After several years in that position, he became European director for CBS in 1937. His broadcasting career began in March, 1938, with Germany's *Anschluss* of Austria. Managing to reach Vienna from Warsaw in time for the arrival of Nazi troops, he received permission to broadcast the story, and did so for the next ten days. Thereafter, he was on the air regularly.

His trademark, the phrase "This Is . . . ," started during the blitz with his celebrated "This Is London" broadcasts, which were published in book form in 1941. Since then he has evolved the radio programs "This Is the News" and "This I Believe."

In 1941 he was honored at a dinner in the United States attended by one thousand guests including high government officials, educators, editors and industrialists. Later, he and Mrs. Murrow were invited to the White House by the late President and Mrs. Roosevelt.

In 1942 Mr. Murrow flew combat missions with the British and United States Air Forces, and covered the North Africa campaign. He was the first war correspondent inside the Nazi concentration camp at Buchenwald.

Mr. Murrow became Vice President and Director of Public Affairs at CBS in 1946 but soon decided he preferred broadcasting to executive work. His postwar news coverage included the Korean War, the wedding and coronation of Queen Elizabeth II, the Berlin crisis leading to the airlift, the election of the British Labour government and the subsequent election of Winston Churchill as well as presidential conventions and elections in the United States.

His television programs "See It Now" and "Person to Person" began in 1951 and 1953, respectively. "See It Now" won the George Foster Peabody Award in 1952. Mr. Murrow also received the Peabody Award in 1943, 1949 and 1954, and the Overseas Press Club Award in 1940, 1948, 1950, 1951 and 1952. King George VI bestowed on him the Order of the British Empire in 1947. Mr. Murrow has received honorary degrees from five colleges and universities.

ALAN MOWBRAY (British Consul, Suez). Born in London in 1893, Alan Mowbray received his theatrical training with a touring company in the provinces. After serving with the British Navy during World War I, he went to the U. S. A. and appeared in several plays on Broadway and on the road for the Theatre Guild.

In 1935 he moved to Hollywood, where he has remained ever since, playing in such films as *Man in Possession, Panama Hattie, Blackbeard the Pirate, Androcles and the Lion* and *The Captain from Castile.*

Mr. Mowbray is a Fellow of the Royal Geographical Society and a member of the Masquers, Players and Overseas Clubs.

JACK OAKIE (Captain, S. S. Henrietta). A native of Sedalia, Missouri, where he was born in 1903, Mr. Oakie started in vaudeville and soon was appearing as a featured comedian in such smash Broadway successes as *Artists and Models, Ziegfeld Follies* and *The Passing Show.*

He came to Hollywood in the late 1920's and appeared in a number of football pictures, then branched out to become one of the most versatile comedians in Hollywood. Among his memorable films are *The Great Dictator, Bowery to Broadway, Hard to Get, Hit the Deck* and *The Fleet's In.*

GEORGE RAFT (Bouncer, Barbary Coast Saloon). Born in New York around the turn of the century, Raft started in show business as a hoofer. He danced in theaters and nightclubs not only in America but in all the capitals of Europe. Later he appeared in a number of Broadway revues, like *Gay Paree,* in song and dance parts.

Lured to Hollywood in 1931, he turned to dramatic acting and made an instantaneous hit in *Scarface.* This success was followed by countless films, including *Bolero, Broadway, Follow the Boys, Johnny Angel, Each Dawn I Die* and *If I Had a Million.*

GILBERT ROLAND (Achmed Abdullah). The son of a prominent bullfighter, Roland was born in Juarez, Mexico, in 1905, and educated in Mexico City. Determined to crash the picture business, he moved to Hollywood where his handsome features and physique quickly won him leading roles in such silent films as *The Dove, Camille* and *The Plastic Age.*

Continuing his career after the change-over to talkies, he has appeared in many films, the most notable of which are *Captain Kidd, The Bullfighter and the Lady, The Treasure of Pancho Villa, The French Line, The Bad and the Beautiful.*

Mr. Roland's career was recently dramatized on "This Is Your Life."

CESAR ROMERO (Henchman of Achmed Abdullah). Born in New York City in 1907, Cesar Romero went to Collegiate and Riverdale Country schools where he studied dramatics.

He made his Broadway debut in 1927 in *Lady Do!* and also appeared as a dancer in nightclubs. Roles in other plays, like *Strictly Dishonorable, Cobra* and *Dinner at Eight,* followed, and for the next few years he remained in the theater.

In 1934, Mr. Romero accepted an offer to play in *The Thin Man* and moved to Hollywood. Recent pictures include *The Captain from Castile, The Beautiful Blonde from Bashful Bend, Lost Continent* and *Vera Cruz.*

FRANK SINATRA (Piano Player, Barbary Coast Saloon). Born in 1918 in Hoboken, New Jersey, Frank Sinatra started out as a newspaper sportswriter. Turning to singing in small night spots, he attracted the attention of Harry James, who offered him a job as soloist with his band. Mr. Sinatra soon left James to take the vocal spot with Tommy Dorsey's orchestra, where his popularity began to grow. Several years later, he left Dorsey to start on his own. A solo engagement at New York's Paramount broke all records at that theater. In January, 1942, he began his own radio program, "Songs by Sinatra," and next became the singing star of Lucky Strike's "Your Hit Parade." He also appeared in New York's smartest nightclubs, including the Wedgwood Room of the Waldorf-Astoria.

In 1943 he made his movie debut in *Higher and Higher*

and a few years later won a Special Academy Award for *The House I Live In,* a short subject on tolerance. In 1951 he went on a strike and refused to continue in musicals. His courage and perseverance paid off two years later when he won the 1953 best supporting player Academy Award for his performance in *From Here to Eternity.*

Recent pictures in which he has appeared include *Not As a Stranger, Guys and Dolls, The Man with the Golden Arm, Johnny Concho, High Society* and, in production, *Pride and the Passion* and *The Joker Is Wild,* the biography of Joe E. Lewis.

 **RED SKELTON (Drunk, Barbary Coast Saloon).** Skelton, who was born in Vincennes, Indiana, in 1914, learned his trade in every possible phase of show business except the legitimate theater. He started out, at the age of ten, as a medicine show midget, later graduated to river showboats, vaudeville turns, burlesque and circus routines.

In 1939, after making a reputation as a radio comic in Chicago, he went to Hollywood to appear in *Having a Wonderful Time.* Among the movies he has made are *Lady Be Good, A Southern Yankee, The Fuller Brush Man* and *Merton of the Movies.*

During World War II, he maintained one of the most popular comedy programs on radio and since 1951 has starred in the equally popular Red Skelton television show.

 **RONALD SQUIRE (Member of Reform Club, London).** An actor with forty-seven years' experience on the British stage, Ronald Squire started out as a journalist. Born in Tiverton, Devonshire, in 1886, the son of an army colonel, he was educated at Wellington College.

His stage debut was made in 1909 in *An Englishman's Home,* and the following year he played in London. He went to Liverpool for the opening of the Repertory Theater, where he appeared in *The Admirable Crichton* and *The Perplexed Husband,* among others. New York audiences have seen him in *Gambler's All* (1917) and *The Sex Fable* (1932).

Mr. Squire produced several plays in the late 1920's, and in 1946 put on *Portrait in Black* in which he portrayed Rupert Marlowe. His many London appearances include *Bulldog Drummond, Dear Brutus, Our Betters, The Last of Mrs. Cheyney, On Approval, Springtime for Henry* and *A Month in the Country.* He toured in *Blithe Spirit* and *While the Sun Shines.*

In 1934 Mr. Squire entered the movies and has appeared in numerous pictures, including *Rocking Horse Winner, Man with a Million* and *No Highway in the Sky.*

 **BASIL SYDNEY (Member of Reform Club, London).** The son of a provincial theater manager, Mr. Sydney was born in St. Osyth, Essex, in 1894. He first appeared on the stage at the age of fifteen, then toured the provinces in such vehicles as *Venture and Vengeance* and *Typhoon.* In 1913 he made his London debut in *Westward Ho!,* and the following year portrayed Claudius in *Hamlet* at the Old Vic.

After an American tour in 1914-15, he joined the Norfolk Regiment. In 1916 he resumed his stage career in *The Double Dealer,* followed by *Ghosts,* and in 1919 played Romeo in *Romeo and Juliet.* The next year he came to the United States, where he stayed for fourteen years, returning twice to London for short periods. In New York and on tour he took the lead in such plays as *Sandro Botticelli, The Devil's Disciple, She Stoops to Conquer, Peer Gynt, Hamlet* and *The Taming of the Shrew.*

Mr. Sydney's first movie was *Romance* in 1920. He did not re-enter motion pictures until 1932. Among the many movies in which he has appeared since then are *Caesar and Cleopatra, Jassy, Hamlet, Treasure Island, Next of Kin* and *The Dam Busters.*

 **HARCOURT WILLIAMS (Aged Steward, Reform Club).** A distinguished veteran of more than fifty years on the stage, Mr. Williams also produced nearly fifty plays at the Old Vic.

Born at Croydon, England, in 1880, Mr. Williams made his first stage appearance at the age of eighteen in Belfast, Ireland, in *Henry V.*

Highlights of a varied career were a season's tour with Ellen Terry in 1903, a number of portrayals of Romeo between 1903 and 1913 and an appearance with John Barrymore in *Hamlet* in 1925. Among his hundreds of plays were Euripides' *Electra, Salomé, The Master Builder, The Three Musketeers, Abraham Lincoln, Napoleon, Mary Stuart, Oliver Cromwell, A Doll's House, Uncle Vanya, The School for Scandal, Rex Oedipus* and *The Lady's Not for Burning.*

Between 1929 and 1934 he was producer at the Old Vic. He has published two books, *Tales from Ebony* (1934) and *Four Years at the Old Vic* (1935).

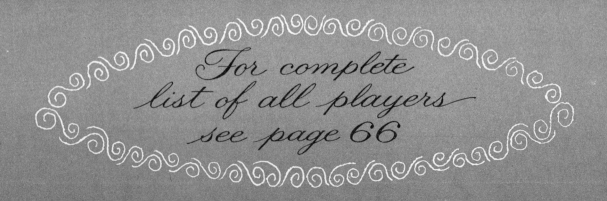
For complete list of all players see page 66

BEHIND THE CAMERA

JULES VERNE. In a life span of seventy-seven years, during which he wrote an estimated eighty stories on travel and exploration, Jules Verne envisioned many things, such as television, remote control, travel by rocket, the helicopter, the atom bomb and then the astounding idea of going *Around the World in Eighty Days.*

Born in Nantes, France, in 1828, Verne studied law but soon gave up its practice to become a writer. Endowed with remarkable imagination and a flair for description, he took his readers on annual voyages of discovery. Guided by the best scientific thinking of the day, Verne's fantasy plumbed the depths of the sea and visited the moon.

A keen student of travel books, Verne wrote his stories without once leaving Nantes. But his accounts of factual incidents were as detailed and accurate as if he had witnessed them himself.

Some of Verne's better-known prophetic romances are, *A Voyage to the Center of the Earth, Twenty Thousand Leagues Under the Sea* and *Five Weeks in a Balloon.* He also wrote librettos for operettas, a comedy in verse, and adapted *Around the World in Eighty Days* and *Michael Strogoff* for the stage. The novels of Jules Verne were forward-looking dreams now come true.

GEORGE MELIES. The prologue to *Around the World in Eighty Days* contains a condensation of the celebrated film *The Trip to the Moon* made in 1902 by George Melies, the magician-artist who was known as the "Jules Verne of the cinema." Although Melies made some 4,000 short movies, today copies of them are collector's items, shown only by art theaters and private collectors. Mr. Todd purchased a copy of *The Trip to the Moon* from the artist's estate.

Melies began his career as a prestidigitator and magician. He was also a skilled artist and caricaturist and is said to be the originator of publicity and advertising films. He created the most charming and humorous fantasies in costuming, setting and action. He was the first to film the French can-can.

In a biography of the artist, the authors, Maurice Bessy and Lo Duca,* note that Melies stated his aim was to produce original films and to avoid "commonplace subjects lacking in artistic interest." According to the authors, Melies "was able to invest an invention which had all the marks of aridity and plainness, which smelled of the laboratory, with the radiance of fantasy and art."

D. W. Griffith once said to Melies, "I owe everything to you," and Charlie Chaplin remarked that the Frenchman "was a veritable alchemist of light."

George Melies, Createur du Spectacle Cinematographique, published in 1945 by Prisma, Paris.

S. J. PERELMAN, Co-Author of the Screenplay. S. J. Perelman, noted for his humorous contributions to *The New Yorker* magazine, approached the writing of the scenario of *Around the World in 80 Days* by a rather curious route. Or perhaps it might be said that he backed into it, having a few years previously published a somewhat unrelated

work entitled *Around the World in Eighty Clichés.*

Born in Brooklyn, New York, Mr. Perelman was educated at Brown University. A brilliant parodist, his stories were immediately accepted by the then popular humor magazines, *Judge* and *College Humor.* He subsequently served for a number of years on their editorial staffs.

In the early 1930's Mr. Perelman migrated to Hollywood to write the screenplays of the Marx brothers' comedies while contributing regularly to *The New Yorker.* Among his published works are *Dawn Ginsbergh's Revenge* and *Look Who's Talking.*

In 1940 he collaborated with his wife on *The Night Before Christmas,* a play concerning a gang of safecrackers who inadvertently tunnel into a delicatessen instead of a bank.

MICHAEL ANDERSON, Director. Michael Anderson was born in London on January 30, 1920, within the sound of the Bow bells (and therefore can claim to be a true "Cockney"). The son of Lawrence Anderson, a noted actor who appeared in the original production of *Berkeley Square,* and the grand-nephew of Mary Anderson, famed American actress, it was only natural that he should gravitate toward show business. He started out as a motion picture actor, in Ian Hay's *The Housemaster,* at the Elstree Studios, but soon decided that he preferred the other side of the camera.

He started at the bottom, as a studio messenger. His rise was steady, from junior assistant director to second to first to, finally, unit manager on Noel Coward's *In Which We Serve.*

During the war, Mr. Anderson was in the British Army, serving much of the time with the Royal Corps of Signals. After being demobilized in 1945, he joined the Two Cities Studio in Denham, working in various capacities as an assistant; but he never lost sight of his objective, which was to become a director, and spent all his spare time in the studio's cutting room, preparing himself.

His first chance came in 1949 when, with Peter Ustinov, he co-directed a film called *Private Angelo.* Following was his first solo job, *Waterfront,* starring Robert Newton (with whom he renewed a professional relationship in *Around the World in 80 Days*). Then, after a couple more British films, he went to Paris to direct *Dial Seventeen,* a French picture. The language was no barrier to him, as he speaks French, Italian and German fluently.

In 1952 Mr. Anderson directed a West End revue. But films were his first love, and he returned to Elstree to direct two pictures for Producer Robert Clark. One of them, *The Dam Busters,* a semi-documentary of the raid during the war on the Ruhr Valley dams by a picked squadron of RAF planes, was awarded the Robertson Memorial Trophy, given annually to the individual, the company or the group doing the most for the RAF's public relations. Starring Richard Todd and Michael Redgrave, the film was a smash hit in England and well received in the United States.

Mr. Anderson was promptly chosen by Peter Rathvon, the American financier who produces films abroad, to direct the screen version of George Orwell's *1984,* starring Edmund O'Brien and Jan Sterling. He was still working on this project when he met Michael Todd. Rathvon released him from the last two weeks of his contract so that he could accept the *Around the World in 80 Days* assignment.

After Mr. Todd saw the first few days' rushes of the footage Anderson shot in England, he signed him for the rest of the picture and also took an option on his services for two other films. Though unassuming in appearance and quiet in manner, he is a sure craftsman, deft in the handling of a scene.

WILLIAM CAMERON MENZIES, Associate Producer. One of the most distinguished men in his field, Mr. Menzies has thirty-five years' experience as an art director, production designer, director and associate producer. Born in New Haven, Connecticut, in 1896, he studied in Scotland and later graduated from Yale University's art school and from the Art Students' League in New York City.

After a brief fling as a commercial illustrator, he entered the motion picture industry in its silent days as a sketch artist for George Fitzmaurice. During World War I he served with the American Expeditionary Force. Soon after the end of the war he went to England to establish the first American-owned studio for Famous Players.

Since then he has divided his time between the two countries and has worked on some of their biggest productions. His movies include *The Thief of Baghdad, For Whom the Bell Tolls, King's Row, Chandu the Magician, Alice in Wonderland, The Adventures of Tom Sawyer, Our Town, The Devil and Miss Jones* and *Address Unknown.*

Mr. Menzies has won two Academy Awards, one for Art Direction of *The Tempest* and *The Dove* in 1928, and the second for Best Dramatic Use of Color in *Gone with the Wind* in 1939.

Mr. Menzies has also directed several motion pictures— *Whip Hand, Drums in the Deep South, The Invaders from Mars* and *The Maze.*

KEVIN O'DONOVAN McCLORY, Associate Producer. To direct the sequences of *Around the World in 80 Days* staged in Paris, the Middle East, Pakistan, Siam, Hong Kong and Japan, Michael Todd selected Kevin McClory, an adventurous young Irishman who flew 44,535 miles in five months to complete his assignment.

Born in Dun Laoghaire, Dublin County, in 1924, McClory was educated at St. Mary's Convent in Ireland, the Harrison Avenue School in the Bronx, New York, and the Finchley Catholic Grammar School in London. His father was Desmond O'Donovan, noted actor of the Irish Players in Dublin. In 1939, at the age of fifteen, he joined the Merchant Marine and four years later the Royal Navy.

After World War II, he worked in the building trade in England and, after a brief period as an actor, joined the British Lion Studios as a member of the sound department. In 1952 he left the film industry to spend fourteen months crossing the Sahara, and went to the Belgian Congo, West Africa, East and South Africa prospecting for tin, trapping crocodiles, snaring parrots and writing.

Returning to London in 1953, he worked as an assistant director with Sir Carol Reed, and prior to his present assignment with Mr. Todd, served as assistant director for John Huston on *Moulin Rouge, African Queen* and *Moby Dick*. While shooting a scene for *Moby Dick*, McClory was carried off by a wounded whale. He was rescued in time to start shooting scenes around the world for Michael Todd.

VICTOR YOUNG, Music. Integrating the authentic music of the countries visited during production into the background score was the task assigned to Victor Young.

Born in Chicago, Illinois, Young was brought up in Warsaw, Poland, where he studied the violin and graduated from the Imperial Conservatory. Returning to this country at the age of twenty, he became musical director for the Balaban & Katz chain of theaters in the Middle West.

Later, coming to Hollywood, he was one of the first composers to introduce original music into film scores. Altogether he has written around 300 themes, including *For Whom the Bell Tolls, The Quiet Man, Golden Boy, The Emperor Waltz, Hold Back the Dawn* and *Golden Earrings*. His popular hits have included "Sweet Sue," "Love Me Tonight," "My Foolish Heart" and "Old Man of the Mountain."

In the realm of serious music, Young has composed such orchestral scores as "Manhattan Concerto," "Arizona Sketches" and "Leaves of Grass," all performed in recent seasons by the San Francisco and Los Angeles Philharmonic Orchestras.

Mr. Young has been nominated for the Academy Award twenty times.

LIONEL LINDON, Photography. The handling of the Todd-AO cameras during production was entrusted to Lionel Lindon, whose facility with the process was so pronounced that the producer promptly offered him a contract to photograph his next two shows.

Born in San Francisco, Lindon attended the local public schools and drifted down to Los Angeles where he got a job in a film laboratory. After learning all there was to know about processing, he joined the Herbert Bosworth studios as an assistant cameraman. Later he moved to the Famous Players-Lasky studio, which is now Paramount Pictures.

During his career as a cinematographer, Lindon has worked with almost every star in the industry, from such silent greats as Rudolph Valentino, Gloria Swanson and Wallace Reed to the present-day champions like Bing Crosby, William Holden and Grace Kelly.

An enterprising craftsman, Lindon was one of the first cameramen to don a diving suit to film underwater sequences and to step on an airplane wing to shoot aerial effects.

Among his outstanding pictures are *Going My Way, Destination Moon* and *Submarine Command*.

JAMES SULLIVAN, Art Direction. Designing the 140 sets constructed for the movie and selecting dozens of location sites used for the exterior sequences was the tremendous assignment given to James Sullivan, the picture's art director.

Born in St. Louis, Missouri, Mr, Sullivan studied architecture at the University of Southern California after graduating fom Polytechnic High in Los Angeles. Associated with several California architectural firms, he worked on the designs of many residences, restaurants and commercial buildings in the Los Angeles area.

He has designed the sets for such memorable films as *Wake of the Red Witch, The Hairy Ape, Tomorrow the World* and *Johnny Guitar*.

ROSS DOWD, Set Decoration. Tracking down the thousands of authentic period pieces used to decorate the picture's 140 studio-constructed sets was the job given to Ross Dowd, head of set decoration.

A native of New York City, Mr. Dowd attended the Loomis School in Connecticut, then studied architecture at the University of Southern California and interior decoration at the Beaux Arts in Paris. Returning to New York after completing his courses in France, he worked with French & Co. as an interior decorator, and later opened his own shop on Madison Avenue.

In 1940, he came to California to do modern houses for Barker Brothers, then joined RKO Studios to work with the Orson Welles-Mercury Theater unit. After doing a series of musicals at 20th Century-Fox, Dowd moved to Paramount where he decorated the sets for dozens of films, both dramatic and musical, including such distinguished pictures as *Come Back, Little Sheba, Little Boy Lost* and *A Foreign Affair*.

MILES WHITE, Costume Designer. Miles White is the internationally known designer who in recent springs has inspired many New York fashions with his lavish Ringling Brothers Circus costumes.

Born in San Francisco, Mr. White majored in art at the University of California in Berkeley, and also studied at the California School of Fine Arts in San Francisco and the Art Student's League in New York City. His first important costuming assignment was for Norman Bel Geddes' ice show, *It Happened on Ice*.

Since then he has been in great demand by theater and motion picture producers. He has received the Antoinette Perry Award for *Bless You All* and *Hazel Flagg*, the Donaldson Award for *Bloomer Girl, High Button Shoes, Gentlemen Prefer Blondes* and *Pal Joey*, and was nominated for Academy Awards for *The Greatest Show on Earth* and *No Business Like Show Business*.

Other Broadway shows for which Mr. White designed the costumes are *Best Foot Forward, Ziegfeld Follies*, the Lunts' *The Pirate, Oklahoma, Carousel, Two's Company, Ankles Aweigh* and, most recently, *Strip for Action*. He also did the costumes for two of Danny Kaye's films, *Up in Arms* and *The Kid from Brooklyn*.

PAUL GODKIN, Choreographer. Mr. Godkin was seen last spring on TV dancing the role which Maurice Evans acted in *The Taming of the Shrew*. His training as a dancer began at the age of seven in Beaumont, Texas. He has toured Europe and the United States with the Ballet Russe, as a soloist in Ballet Theater and as a concert performer.

Mr. Godkin served with the U. S. Navy for three and one-half years and participated in several Pacific invasions. Once during a lull in the fighting, he put on a musical show aboard his ship.

His first professional choreographic effort, in 1948, served also to introduce him to Michael Todd. It was a ballet, "Willie the Weeper," arranged for ANTA's *Ballet Ballads*, which had been commissioned by Mr. Todd. The ballet received rave notices from the critics, and since then Mr. Godkin has been in demand as a choreographer as well as dancer. In 1953 he arranged the dances for an international revue in Paris which starred Colette Marchand and Maurice Chevalier.

JOSEPH KANE, Sound. A native of Pontiac, Illinois, Joseph Kane was attending the University of Notre Dame when America entered World War I. He left college to join the Army. After the armistice, he worked as a radio operator on private yachts and merchant ships, touching most of the ports in the seven seas. But a chilling experience in the ice fields off the coast of Norway sent him scurrying to Los Angeles, where he took a landlubber job with radio station, KNX.

In 1928 he joined Warner Brothers, and worked as sound mixer on a number of that studio's early talking pictures. He was later associated with both the East and West Coast studios of Western Electric, turning out as many as 150 pictures a year.

During World War II, Mr. Kane worked for the Bell Laboratories in England, promoting the use of radar for the defense of London and for pinpointing the drop zones of invading paratroopers.

After an interesting experience in Rome, recording the voices of the Sistine Chapel Choir, he returned to Hollywood to work in the new Todd-AO medium on the dubbing of *Oklahoma!*

LEE ZAVITZ, Special Effects. Neither rain nor snow nor fire nor smoke nor fog ever stayed Lee Zavitz on his appointed rounds in cinema special effects, but he had to call on all his years of experience to complete the requirements for *Around the World in 80 Days*.

Zavitz was born in Mount Vernon, Virginia. After completing his education he worked in coal mines and learned a great deal about explosives. When he moved to Hollywood at the age of eighteen, it seemed only natural that he should put this knowledge to work in the film studios where quantities of war pictures were then being made.

Employed by Fox, he started what is now known as the special effects department in the studios. In charge of all the physical aspects of a picture, including explosions, breakaway construction and miniatures, he oversaw the burning of Atlanta in *Gone with the Wind*, the destruction of the French fleet in *That Hamilton Woman* and the battering of the South Sea island in *The Hurricane*.

PERCY GUTH, Vice President and General Manager. Thirty-two years' experience with half a dozen motion picture studios qualified Percy Guth for the post of Vice President and General Manager of the Michael Todd Company, Inc., whose initial film is *Around the World in 80 Days*.

Born and brought up in St. Louis, Missouri, Guth attended the public schools there. After graduating from Washington University, he served in the U. S. Navy during World War I, then was associated with the U. S. Railroad Administration as a traveling auditor. Later he worked as a statistician for the U. S. Steel Corporation.

After service with the Great Western Oil Refining Company as assistant to the president, he joined F.B.O. studio in Hollywood in a business capacity. Subsequently, he held business and production managerial positions with a number of other studios and independent companies, including Walter Wanger Productions, 20th Century-Fox, British & Dominion Films, Ltd., International Pictures, RKO and Universal-International.

SAMUEL LAMBERT, Executive Assistant. Mr. Lambert was born in St. Louis, Missouri, in 1909. He began his career in show business as a chorus boy in the St. Louis Municipal Opera. After five summers he was made stage manager for the opera company. In 1930 J. J. Shubert asked him to come to New York as a stage manager, and during his nine years with the Shuberts he rose from stage manager to director to theater manager.

In 1939 he began a long association with Michael Todd, staging first *The Hot Mikado.* He continued as general stage manager for the producer's long series of Broadway hits, in 1944 overseeing five Todd shows, *The Would-Be Gentleman, Hamlet, Up in Central Park, Mexican Hayride* and *January Thaw.*

Mr. Lambert in 1947 struck out on his own as a producer. His shows include *Hold It,* starring Red Buttons; *All for Love* with the Hartmans and Bert Wheeler; and the hit musical version of Tarkington's *Seventeen.*

At the start of tests of the Todd-AO process, he returned to serve as unit manager for Mr. Todd on all the tests prior to the shooting of *Oklahoma!* When the Michael Todd Company, Inc., was organized in 1955, Mr. Lambert became executive assistant of the new company.

He is a member of the Motion Picture Academy of Arts and Sciences.

SCHUYLER A. SANFORD, Todd-AO Consultant. When in 1953 the American Optical Company took on the development of the revolutionary Todd-AO camera process, it asked for an experienced Hollywood camera technician to work with its staff of scientists and engineers in an advisory capacity, and for this meticulous job Michael Todd recommended Schuyler Sanford.

Born in Columbus, Ohio, Mr. Sanford brought to the American Optical Company laboratories nearly twenty years of experience with motion picture equipment. Starting in the Paramount camera department as a film loader, he worked up from assistant cameraman to operator to technician. In World War II, he received a commission in the Air Force and was in charge of motion picture photographic training.

After spending nearly two years with American Optical on the development of the Todd-AO cameras, in 1954 he acted as technical consultant on the production of *Oklahoma!*

Mr. Sanford is now the General Manager of the Todd-AO motion picture division, which has its headquarters in Hollywood.

FRANK FOX, Unit Manager. Frank Fox was the man entrusted with the thousands of details connected with the business end of the production.

Born in Brownsville, Texas, Fox graduated from high school at the age of thirteen and attended college in Texas and Mexico City. After living for several years south of the border, he moved to Hollywood. There he joined Warner Brothers in the capacity of script clerk, eventually working his way up to dialogue director and assistant director.

In 1950, he returned to Mexico to work for the Mexican film companies as a unit manager and also to represent the late Leonard Goldstein, an independent producer. Coming back to Hollywood in 1955, he took on the assignment of unit manager for the Michael Todd show.

SAUL BASS, Screen Credits Designer. Because of the exceptionally large cast and production staff, Mr. Todd realized that the presentation of screen credits in the ordinary manner would be a long and tedious affair. Seeking the unusual, Mr. Todd decided to animate the screen credits and present them in an epilogue. Saul Bass, well-known art director and graphics designer, was the logical choice to execute this idea.

Mr. Bass was born in New York City thirty-six years ago. He studied at the Art Student's League under Howard Trafton and at Brooklyn College under Gyorgy Kepes. For a time he freelanced and worked as art director for various advertising agencies in New York. In 1946 Mr. Bass went to Los Angeles to direct art activities for Buchanan & Company in their West Coast offices. Four years later he joined Foote, Cone & Belding in Los Angeles as art director.

Since 1952 he has functioned as designer and consultant for advertising agencies. In addition to advertisements in periodicals, his work includes package design, merchandise and point-of-sale displays, exhibitions, direct mail pieces and the complete redesign of company stationery. But he is known to moviegoers as the man who has made the presentation of screen titles and credits interesting. His first opportunity in this field was *Carmen Jones,* for which he created the motif of the rose surrounded by a flame which flickered through the entire list of credits, accompanied by the music of Bizet. Other pictures for which Mr. Bass has designed titles and credits are *The Seven Year Itch, The Big Knife, The Man with the Golden Arm* and *Trapeze.*

The designer's work has often received awards and special recognition from the New York and Los Angeles Art Directors Club, the National Association of Lithographers, the American Institute of Graphic Arts and other organizations. Examples of his designs have appeared in many art shows, including the International Poster Exhibition at The Hague in 1956, the International Graphic Arts Exhibition in London (1956), a one-man show in San Francisco (1954), the permanent collection at the Museum of Modern Art in New York and in "Printing and Design in America," a traveling exhibition shown in Europe and South America in 1953.

WHAT IS TODD-AO?

TODD-AO is the cumulation of Michael Todd's dream and the execution by a small army of scientists at the American Optical Company at Southbridge, Massachusetts, supervised by a man who has spent a lifetime translating dreams into reality—Dr. Brian O'Brien.

Around the World in 80 Days is the second film to be made in the revolutionary Todd-AO process. This is the gigantic, wide-screen system pioneered by Michael Todd and developed by Dr. Brian O'Brien and the 100 engineers and craftsmen of the American Optical Company, with Schuyler Sanford serving as advisory camera technician. The process scored a huge success in Rodgers & Hammerstein's *Oklahoma!* and promises to be even better by the time *Around the World in 80 Days* reaches the screen, as numerous refinements and improvements have since been made.

Todd-AO is not merely wide screen. It is large screen and wide angle. Todd-AO motion pictures are photographed on film that is 65 mm. in width — wider than the conventional 35 mm. film used in all other wide-film processes. Both negative and prints are made on Eastman Color film, which is processed by Technicolor Laboratories, Hollywood, California.

On the same order as Cinerama, but vastly superior, since it is photographed with only one camera and projected with only one machine instead of three, Todd-AO gives the spectator an extraordinary feeling of audience participation.

Completely new cameras had to be built for the system. They are approximately the size of a Mitchell, but have a slightly larger head and wider film magazines to accommodate the larger 65 mm. negative. The wider film allows greater flexibility and degree of clarity. The 65 mm. picture frame is three and one-half times the area of the standard 35 mm. frame. Where there are four sprocket holes on either side of the conventional 35 mm. film frame, the 65 mm. Todd-AO frame has five sprocket holes. Another feature is the higher speed of film travel. Camera speed has been stepped up from the conventional twenty-four frames per second to thirty, which tends to smooth out action on the larger screen.

As with conventional motion picture cameras, the Todd-AO takes a range of lenses of different sizes; but unlike the lenses used on 35 mm. motion picture cameras, which vary in focal length, the Todd-AO lenses are classified according to angle of coverage. Thus Todd-AO has a selection of four lenses that cover everything from a closeup to distant scenic shots. These range from the huge 128 degree "bugeye" wide-angle lens—so called because of its enormous front element—down through the 64, 48 and 37 degree (angle of coverage) lenses.

According to Robert Surtees, Todd-AO is a much better approach to wide-screen film production and exhibition than any other new process, because of the overall larger negative area of the Todd-AO 65 mm. film. Moreover, he says, by projecting prints made on 65 mm. film, a far superior picture quality results on the screen.

"From the standpoint of optics alone," Robert Surtees, Director of Photography for *Oklahoma!*, said, "Todd-AO is a superior picture process. The proportion of the screened image is better, too. In short, Todd-AO is the epitome of perfection for the director of photography. From the point of composition Todd-AO presents a much better format—one that affords greater compositional latitude for the cameraman and enables him to do a great many things pictorially that he has never been able to do in 35 mm. with the three by four format.

"With Todd-AO," Surtees continued, "we don't have to work so close to the players, big closeups are better and we don't have to worry about space at the sides as is the case with CinemaScope."

The origination and development of Todd-AO called for a complete revolution in equipment design, from the camera down to the splicers. Even the sound recording equipment had to be completely redesigned. A new high-fidelity system is employed that involves seven channels—six sound channels plus one control. These channels add 5 mm. in width to the film, so that the width of the release prints is 70 mm.

The Phillips Electric Company of Holland designed and constructed the Todd-AO projectors.

The Phillips company recently completed a revolutionary new "universal" projector for theaters. It takes both 35 mm. and 70 mm. films interchangeably, enabling an exhibitor to screen motion pictures in every format that is presently available without the need for investing in dual projection equipment. The changeover from 35 mm. to 70 mm. is accomplished simply by flicking a switch and twisting one or two dials.

Who's Who

Cast

Featured Players

UNITED STATES

Richard Aherne
Philip Ahn
Roy Aversa
Frank Baker
Alex Ball
John Benson
Leon Bouvard
Donald Brown
Ollie Brown
Theona Bryant
J. W. Burr
Robert Cabal
Al Cavens
Fred Cavens
Shih Hung Choy
Neil Collins
Cecil Combs
Louis Cortina
Ashley Cowan
Roy Darmour
Maria Delgardo
Anna de Linsky
Amapola del Vando
Leslie Denison
Clint Dorrington
Ed Edmonson
Carli D. Elinor
Duke Fishman
Frances Fong
Raoul Freeman
Tom Fujiwara
Joseph Garcio
Harry Gilette
Joseph Glick
Arthur Gould-Porter
Bernard Gozier
Ralph Grosh
Chuck Hamilton
Mahgoub Hanaf (Galli Galli)
Doc Harnett
Chester Hayes
Tex Holden
David B. Hughes
Joanne Jones
Paul King
Walter Kingsford
Ben Knight
Katy Koury
Freddie Letuli
Weaver Levy
Richard Loo
Manuel Lopez

Joan Lora
Keye Luke
Robert McNulty
Casey MacGregor
D. Ellsworth Manning
Dewey Manning
Harry Mayo
Lorion Miller
Maria Monay
Jack Mulhall
Robert Okazaki
Manuel Paris
James Porter
Satini Puailoa
Amando Rodriguez
George Russell
Jim Salisbury
Sohi Shannon
Bhogwan Singh
Alvin Slaight
Fred O. Somers
Owen Kyoon Song
Ward Thompson
Philip Van Zandt
Frank Vessels, Jr.
Al Walton
Richard Wessel
Robert Whitney
Kathryn Wilson
Thomas Quon Woo

LONDON

Ronald Adams
R. Brodie
Patrick Cargill
Campbell Cotts
Felix Fetton
Cameron Hall
Maria Hanson
Roddy Hughes
Frederick Leister
N. Macowen
Frank Royd
Bill Shine
Janet Sterke
Trubshaw
Richard Wattis

Stuntmen

Reginald C. Armor, Jr.
Paul Baxley
Jerry Brown
Bob Burrows
Dick Crockett
Don Cunningham
Mario Dacal
Robert Folkerson
Bob Gordon

Saul Gorss
Joseph Goss
Tex Holden
Charles Horvath
Ace Clyde Hudkins
Alexander Jackson
Bert LeBaron
Boyd Morgan
Charles Mosley
Edwin Parker
Gilbert Perkins
Walter Pietila
Allen D. Pinson
George Ross, Jr.
Frosty Royse
Danny Sands
Audrey Saunders
Raymond Saunders
Russell Saunders
Clint Sharp
George Spotts
Wayne Van Horn
Dale Van Sickle
Frank Vincent
Bill White
Louis Williams
Bud Wolfe

Stand-ins

UNITED STATES

Wanda Brown
Leslie Raymaster
Ed Scarpa
Virginia Whitmire
John Zuniga
Antonion Gutierrez
Esteban Gutierrez

EXTRAS, HOLLYWOOD

Abbas, Abdullah
Abbey, Leo
Abraham, Charles
Ace, Dinah
Ace, Rosemary
Ackerman, Boyd
Acosta, Panchita
Adams, Francis
Adams, Jesse
Addar, David
Agawa, George
Aquilar, Ernest
Ahuna, Benny
Akahoshi, Fred
Albert, Cárolos
Alden, Gladys
Aldrich, Fred
Alegata, Emil

Ali, Kurpan
Allen, Lorey
Alonzo, Sally
Alvarado, Lupe
Ames, Dick
Angelo, August
Angelo, William
Arbogast, Ed
Ardell, Gene
Aredas, Danny
Armstrong, Ray
Arnett, Ray
Arnold, Larry
Ash, Russell
Asher, Eula
Astor, Gertrude
Astran, Edward
Atsumo, George
Auelua, Besmark
Auld, Aggie
Austin, Irene
Awai, Kaz
Aziko, Sande

Bacon, Walter
Bai, Rama
Bain, Al
Baird, Leah
Ball, Alex
Bancroft, Benjie
Bara, Ralph
Barber, Dick
Barbier, Bertha
Barker, Beverly
Barone, Olga
Barroga, Salvador
Barry, Robert
Bates, Merril F.
Batten, Mary Ellen
Baucine
Bauer, Angelina
Beach, Brandon
Beattie, Elena
Beday, Eugene
Bell, Ivan
Benda, Helena
Bender, Eleanor
Bernhart, Norma D.
Berumen, Alfred
Betz, Audrey
Big, Ongyue
Birchfiel, Bobby
Bissutti, Cathy Ann
Bissutti, Richard
Blagoi, George
Blagoi, Tina
Blanco, Eumenio

Blank, Oscar
Blong, Rosemary
Bloom, George
Bloom, Phil
Bloom, William
Bond, Toni
Bordman, Paul
Borget, Olga
Borzage, Dan
Bouvard, Leon
Boyne, Hazel
Bradley, Virginia
Bramucci, Mario
Bray, Kahala
Breneman, John
Brengk, Ernest
Brischof, Kenneth
Brown, Donald
Brown, Mildred
Brown, Wanda
Bruggeman, George
Brunner, Phyllis
Bruno, Helen
Buckley, Joan
Buen, Al
Burgess, Jane
Burgess, Ted
Burns, Betty
Burrows, Bob
Busch, Paul
Buscola, Guy
Cabeen, Boyd
Cahn, Eugene
Calm, Allen
Cameron, Ann
Cameron, Joyce
Carboni, John
Carpenter, Fred
Carr, Mick
Carson, Kit
Carter, Dick
Cartina, Louis
Carveith, Gordon
Casabian, Danny
Caspari, Marlene L.
Castneda, Perta
Cavalieri, Steve
Cefali, Bert
Ceniceros, Frank
Chan, Dorothy
Chan, Douglas
Chan, Eugene
Chan, Jowe
Chan, Lum
Chan, Mary
Chan, Ronald
Chan, Spencer

Cameo Stars

CHARLES BOYER	M. Gasse, clerk, Thomas Cook, Paris
JOE E. BROWN	Station master, Fort Kearney
MARTINE CAROL	Girl in railroad station, Paris
JOHN CARRADINE	Col. Proctor, San Francisco politico
CHARLES COBURN	Clerk, Hong Kong steamship office
RONALD COLMAN	Official, Great Indian Peninsular Railway
MELVILLE COOPER	Steward, *R.M.S. Mongolia*
NOEL COWARD	Roland Hesketh-Baggott, manager of London employment agency
FINLAY CURRIE	Member of Reform Club
REGINALD DENNY	Inspector, Bombay Police
ANDY DEVINE	First Mate, *S.S. Henrietta*
MARLENE DIETRICH	Owner, Barbary Coast saloon
LUIS MIGUEL DOMINGUIN	Bullfighter, Spain
FERNANDEL	Coachman, Paris
SIR JOHN GIELGUD	Foster, ex-employee of Fogg
HERMIONE GINGOLD	Tart, London
JOSE GRECO	Dancer, Cave of the Seven Winds
SIR CEDRIC HARDWICKE	Sir Francis Cromarty, Bombay-Calcutta train
TREVOR HOWARD	Fallentin, member of Reform Club
GLYNIS JOHNS	Tart, London
BUSTER KEATON	Train conductor, San Francisco to Fort Kearney
EVELYN KEYES	Tart, Paris
BEATRICE LILLIE	Leader of Revivalist group, London
PETER LORRE	Japanese steward, *S.S. Carnatic*
EDMUND LOWE	Chief Engineer, *S.S. Henrietta*
A. E. MATTHEWS	Billiard player, Reform Club
MIKE MAZURKI	Drunk, Hong Kong dive
COL. TIM McCOY	Commander U. S. Cavalry, Fort Kearney
VICTOR McLAGLEN	Helmsman, *S.S. Henrietta*
JOHN MILLS	London cabby
ALAN MOWBRAY	British consul, Suez
ROBERT MORLEY	Ralph, a Governor of the Bank of England
JACK OAKIE	Captain, *S.S. Henrietta*
GEORGE RAFT	Bouncer, Barbary Coast saloon
GILBERT ROLAND	Achmed Abdullah
CESAR ROMERO	Henchman of Achmed Abdullah
FRANK SINATRA	Piano player, Barbary Coast saloon
RED SKELTON	Drunk, Barbary Coast saloon
RONALD SQUIRE	Member of Reform Club
BASIL SYDNEY	Member of Reform Club
HARCOURT WILLIAMS	Aged steward, Reform Club

Chan, Suey
Chan, Wong Hing
Chang, Pauline
Chapman, Irene
Chefe, Jack
Cherie, Huaplala
Cherney, Dick
Chillson, Fon
Chinn, May
Chirva, Nina
Chissell, N. Kid
Chon, Lee
Chow, Margarite
Christian, Beulah
Chu, Elaine Leemoi
Chueng, Howard M.
Cui, Kui Sau
Chun, Wong
Chung, Bing Yee
Chung, Jane
Chung, Sue Fawn
Cichy, Martin
Cirillo, Michael
Clark, Richard Dale
Clifford, Mary Loue
Clinton, Walter
Cokes, Bud
Collins, Neil
Colombet, Louise
Conde, Anthony M.
Connors, Kathy
Conrad, Connie
Contreras, Miguel
Cooper, Chabling
Corbett, Joan
Cornell, Wilson

Corral, Dolores
Correa, Barbara
Couch, William J.
Courtland, Theresa
Craft, Lynne
Cristo, Paul
Cruz, Catalina
Culp, Stuart W.
Curtis, Dorothy
Cutler, Max

Dadisman, Gloria
Dalbrook, Ruth
Damron, Roy
Dano, Anita Louise
Dantez, Edmund
Daquila, Lawrence
Darling, Theresa
Darmour, Roy
Das, Eddie
Date, Richard
Davidoff, Serafin
Davidson, Jack
Davies, Jack
Davis, Jack
Dayo, Robert
Dea, Gloria
Deane, Diana
Deangelo, Joseph
Deauville, John
Decarlo, Louise
Dee, Helen
Deena
Deer, George
Degioia, Douglas
Deglar, Maria

DeLacey, Denice
Delgado, John
Delgado, Maria
Delinsky, Anna
Dell, La Verne
Delrio, Jack
Delva, Rosita
De Medici, Rod
De Meo, Angelo
Dennis, Emory
Dennis, Gil
Denny, Harry
Desmond, Kathleen
Detolly, Lala
De Valle, Gabriel
Deward, Gloria
Dewitt, Angela
Dhillon, Maya Kaur
Dialon, Marilyn
Dillard, Sterling
Dime, James
Dix, Franklin
Dodds, Edward Gary
Domasin, Dolores
Dominguez, Robert
Dominguez, William
Donaldson, Barbara
Donelley, William
Dorrington, Clint
Dorsey, Diane
Dorsey, Julie
Dougherty, Joe
Dowling, Al
Dowling, Dan
Downs, Jack
Drabin, Fanny

Drabin, Morris
Drake, Barbara
Drake, Helen
Drake, John
Drapean, Dewey
Draper, Joseph
Dublin, Darren
Du Bois, Alfonso
Duff, Harry
Dulac, Arthur
Dulaine, Robert
Dumont, Gordon
Dunbar, Charles
Dupont, Renald
Duran, Lawrence
Duray, William
Durfee, Minta
Duval, Andre K.
Duval, Hedi
Dyer, Bob
Dyer, Joan
Dylong, Mitchell

Earl, Elaine
Edell, Ina
Eddy, Everett L.
Egan, Michka
Egna, Anita
Elinor, Carli D.
Elliott, Jerry
Ellis, Jack
Elmore, Richard
Eloff, John
Emery, Calvin
Eng, Ronald
Enriquez, Helen

Erickson, Frank
Erickson, Maude
Erwin, Madge
Esquembre, Miguel
Estorres, Marcello
Evans, Bob
Evans, Harry
Evans, Joe
Faber, Henry
Fahrney, Dr. F. W.
Fakato, James
Farfan, Antonio
Farnum, Franklin
Farr, Amir
Farrell, Margaret
Fay, Joe
Faylauer, Adolph
Felix, Art
Fillion, Tony
Findon, Walter
Finn, Samuel
Fioff, John
Fiore, Carlo
Fishman, Duke
Flowers, Bess
Flynn, Ray
Fogel, Charles
Foley, Gene Hunter
Folkerson, Bob
Fong, Clarence
Fong, Dick
Fong, Richard G.
Fong, Sam
Fong, Yut Man
Fontes, Raymond
Forrest, Otto

Foster, Helen
Fox, John
Francis, Harold
Franco, Jess
Freeburg, Oscar
Freeman, Raoul
Freibrun, Milton
Friedman, Wilma
Fritz, John
Fritz, Shela
Frommer, Ben
Fuentes, Virginia
Fujinani, Janice
Fukdo, Koshihiro
Fuller, Jay
Funo, Sumi
Furberg, Curt
Furukawa, John
Furukawa, M.
Furukawa, Yoneka

Gainey, Carol Ann
Gainey, Michael
Galic, Juliana
Gallagher, A.
Gallagher, Al
Gamboa, Elias
Garcia, Charles
Garcia, Capt. Fernan
Carcia, Israel
Garcio, Joseph
Garrison, Diana
Garvin, Robert
Gates, Mark
Gee, Edward
Gee, June
Gee, Toc Yee
Gee, Wong Kim
Geer, Wayne
Gegna, Anita
Generaux, Carine A.
George, John
Gerard, Jay
Germane, Rudolph
Gibson, Curly
Gilbert, Elaine
Gilbert, Joe
Gill, Leon
Gillette, Harry
Gin, H. D.
Gin, Njon Tuey
Ginn, May
Ginn, Noreen
Ginn, Stephen, Jr.
Ginoza, Kay
Git, Wong
Glasson, Howard C.
Gleason, Mary Ellen
Glennie, Betty J.
Glick, Joseph
Glory, June
Godderis, Albert
Gold, Joe
Goldman, Roy
Gomez, Angela
Gong, Mar Suey
Gong, Quon
Gonzales, Soledad
Gonzalez, Armando
Gonzalez, Alex
Gonzalez, Carmen
Gonzalez, Charles
Gonzalez, Fernando
Gonzalez, James
Goode, Allen
Gooding, Alora
Goodrich, Verne
Gook, Lee Teu
Gordon, Eve
Gordon, Richard
Gordon, Ruth
Gotanda, Mickey
Goto, Oxy
Goulet, Violet
Graeff, Ann
Graeff, Betty
Graeff, Rita
Graeff, William Jr.
Graffeo, Joan
Graham, Hershel
Grant, Grace
Gratton, Valerie
Gray, Dolly
Gray, Don
Greco, Elenora Norina
Greco, Suzanne
Greene, David
Greenwood, David
Gribbel, Karla

Groom, B. Pat
Grosh, Ralph
Groves, Sei
Groves, Sei Jeri
Groves, Victor
Grubb, Edward
Guard, Kit
Guerin, Tenmana
Guerra, Edward A.
Guerra, Jesus
Gustafson, Marilyn
Gustine, Paul
Gutierrez, Georgina
Ha, Edward
Hack, Herman
Haines, Robert
Hafl, Betty
Hall, Stuart
Hamilton, Chuck
Hannan, Chick
Haro, Maria
Harr, Silver
Harris, Major Sam
Hart, Louis G.
Hasagawa, James
Hashimoto, George
Hashimoto, Gus
Hashimoto, Harry
Haskell, Al
Hastings, Lauren
Hayden, William
Hayes, Chester
Heaney, Frank
Heard, Charles
Heart, Shirley
Henjum, Bonnie
Hennecke, Charles
Hennecke, Clarence
Hennes, Robert
Hensen, Tars
Hickman, George
Hicks, Charles
Higa, George
Hikawa, Sue
Hing, Jenny
Hiraga, Yoshio
Hiroshige, Kimiko
Hisamune, Hiroshi
Ho, Fun
Hoagland, Harlan
Hock, Lee Yuen
Hohamura, Yoshyo
Holden, Tex
Holmes, Stuart
Holtby, Syd
Hom, Yee Jock
Homabe, Kenny
Homano, Midori
Hong, Lee Kim
Hood, Janice
Hopf, Hans R.
Horan, James
Hoskin, John
Houghton, Shep
Hovey, Ken
Howe, Gladys
Hoy, Lee Yuen
Hubbard, Madelon
Hudkins, Clyde
Huff, Warren
Humphrey, Tom
Hunt, Frank

Iguchi, S.
Iguchi, Yoneo
Iino, Joe
Ikari, Taruko
Ikida, Kazuo
Imamura, Kay
Imazaki, Omaru
Impolito, John
Inez, David
Ingraham, Vi
Irvin, Leona
Isbell, Merrill C.
Ishibashi, Yoshio
Ishikura, Tom
Ishimatsu, Ray
Ito, Kinuko
Iwaki, Roy

Jackler, Jacqueline
Jackson, Diane
Jackson, Marjorie
Jaffe, Allen
James, Charles
James, Idell
James, Robert
Jan, Mary

Janadas, Sushila
Jann, Gerald
Janssen, William A.
Jarvis, Dolly
Jeffers, Michael
Jerrae, Joan
Jewett, Robert
Joe, Dee Ho
Johnson, Edgar W.
Johnson, Leroy
Johnstone, Dick
Joko, Todd
Jones, A. Winfield
Jones, Freda
Jones, Joanne
Jones, Myra
Jones, Sallie
Journeay, Madge
Joyer, Raymond
Jung, S. S.

Kajikawa, Fred
Kakumi, Al
Kam, Gee Toy
Kamaka, Yukimi
Kameshita, Joe
Kamijama, Stanley
Kanae, Mary
Kane, Ken
Kane, Madelynne
Kaneshire, Morris
Karaki, Mamie
Karels, Harvey C.
Karlin, Bopeep
Kashaka, Harumi
Kato, Ken
Katsuhiro, George
Kawashima, George
Kawashima, Tak
Keeler, Sugar Willi
Kekipi, Valentine
Kelley, Jodi
Kelly, Joan
Kennerly, Fannie
Kenney, Jack Heavy
Kent, Eleanor
Kern, Johnny
Key, Joseph Gee
Kila, Allan
Kim, John
King, Anita
King, Brian
King, Grace
King, Paul
Kinnon, Judith A.
Kinoshita, Ken
Kito, Shinya
Kleven, Max
Kloss, Marlene
Kneeland, Frank
Kollberg, William J.
Kong, King
Konno, Bob
Kono, James
Koshi, Harry
Kouchi, Roy
Koury, Kay
Koyama, Akira
Koyama, Tom
Kress, Gladys
Kruger, Paul
Krupnick, Jack
Kum, Jo Ngau
Kunde, Ann
Kushinaejo, Wally
Kusumajo, Wallace
Kuwashige, George
Kuwashige, Sumiyo
Kwong, Jeung Lai

Laceman, Lita
Lacy, Paul
Ladd, Clyde
Lafayette, Jeanne
Lamarr, Richard
Lamb, Laura
Lamont, Connie
Landrum, Cherokee
Lane, Frank
Lane, Warren
Lang, James
Lagrange, Webster
Lara, Frances
Laraneta, Manuel
Larson, Jean
Latzke, Lydia
Lavere, June
Lax, Gustave
Lazelle, Park

Lee, B. M.
Lee, Bik Yuk
Lee, Esther Ying
Lee, Fee Loon
Lee, Foo
Lee, Gee Sho
Lee, Harold
Lee, Helen
Lee, Jack
Lee, Margaret
Lee, Nelson
Lee, Ng Jung
Lee, Norman
Lee, Richard Goon
Lee, Teng Kem
Lee, Tommy
Lee, Virginia
Legneur, Charles
Lem, Lewellyn
Leng, Christopher
Leng, Marian
Leng, Marrilee
Lennox, Jeanne
Leonard, Frank
Leonard, Peggy
Leonard, Rita
Leone, Johnny
Leong, Rose
Leroy, Harry
Leroy, Lillian
Letulli, Freddie
Leviness, Carl
Lew, Mabel
Lew, Shirley
Lewin, William H.
Lewis, John
Lexaber, Eleanor
Leyton, James
Lichter, Baron
Liggett, Amelia
Lim, David
Lim, Gin
Lim, Sing
Lindsay, Geraldine
Ling, Quong
Ling, Yee Suey
Lockwood, King
Logue, Dale
Long, James
Loo, Kwong You
Look, Lee Duck
Look, Tu Duck
Lopez, Caroline
Lopez, Marco
Lopez, Richard
Lora, Joan
Loredo, Marie
Lorraine, Robert L.
Louie, Billie
Louie, Donald
Louie, James
Louie, Marygold
Louie, Wilbert
Loureau, Louise
Lowe, Harry, Jr.
Lue, Wai
Lum, Cop
Lum, David
Lum, Pauline
Lvarado, Lupe

Ma, Bessie
MacCallister, Bruce
MacDonell, Duncan
Macomber, Ann
Macy, Michael M.
Madamba, Celeste
Madlener, Ralph
Maeshiro, T.
Maeua, Roy
Malasig, Guadelope
Malis, Cy
Malyama, Shoji
Manues, Max
Mansfield, Tela
Marievsky, Joseph
Marintz, Ramon
Mariunsky, Joseph
Marlin, John
Marlin, Rena
Marriott, Sandee
Marshall, Gloria
Marsico, Joseph
Martinez, Carlos
Martin, Rickey
Martin, Thomas F.
Mascari, Mary D.
Masson, Rudy
Mathews, Nita

Mathews, Peter
Matsumoto, Corky
Matsutani, John
Mauda, Mack
May, Dorothy
Mayo, Harry
Mayon, George
McAvoy, Ila
McCall, Angelita
McCall, David O.
McCarthy, Glen
McClure, Frank L.
McComas, Glen
McCrady, Robert
McElroy, Robert F.
McGuire, Donald
McGurk, Bob
McIntyre, Lanie
McKaye, Sylvia
McKim, Dorcas
McNamara, Rowena
Meada, William
Medina, Rudolph
Meeker, Russell
Melesch, Marie
Merman, Ann
Merrill, Tommy
Mides, Sam A.
Miller, Harold
Mills, Frank
Milton, Robert
Mishimoto, Tom
Mitchell, Lennie
Mitsunaga, Tameo
Miyaji, Mary
Miyamoto, Henry
Miyarahara, Helen
Mizukami, Luther
Mizushima, Irene
Mizushima, Sam
Mohlmann, James, Jr.
Mojave, King
Molina, Joe
Monahan, William
Monsour, Marion
Mook, Beverly
Moon, Lee Kai
Moore, Earl
Mora, Zelinda
Moratz, Ralph
Morelli, Ernest
Morelli, Michael
Moreno, Linda
Morgan, Cline
Morgan, Patricia
Moriarty, Evelyn
Morita, Thomas
Moriyama, Shiegeyo
Morris, Patricia
Morton, Charles
Motonada, Shirley
Motowaki, Kai
Moy, Man Ho
Mullen, Thomas
Murakami, Inez
Murakami, Jan
Murgi, Sol
Murphy, Joe
Murray, Tessie
Murray, Thomas
Musso, Michael
Myers, George
Myers, Stevie
Nag, Satya Nanda
Nagai, Frank
Nagai, Kisaduro
Nakado, Hiro
Nakado, Kico
Nakado, Kisabaro
Nakado, Tsunesuki
Nakai, Joe
Nakamaura, Charles
Nakamura, Mary
Nakano, Fred
Nakashima, Kay
Nakasoni, Ken
Naley, Frank E.
Nardelli, George
Navarro, Aurora
Nelson, Myra
Neves, Augie
Newmark, Stewart
Newton, H. B.
Newton, Irving Fig
Ng, Ngai Foo
Ng, Woo Shee
Nickum, Charles
Nind, William H.
Ninura, Keiko

Nishida, Shizuko
Nishihar, Bob
Noda, Roy
Noe, Lynn
Nordon, Joseph
Northpole, Anton
Norton, Barry
Nuell, Faye
Nunez, Daniel

O'Brien, Kathy
O'Brien, William H.
O'Carroll, June
Ock, Jeong Wah
O'Connell, Peggy Mae
Odell, Kent
O'Donnell, Patricia
Ogawa, George
Ogawa, Judy
Ogawa, Yasu
O'Grady, Monty
Ohashi, Sati
Ohye, Joe
Okazaki, Robert
Okazaki, Tak
Oklander, Ruth
Okusu, George
O'Laughlin, Agnes
Olen, Bob
Olson, Adrian
Olson, Andra
O'Malley, Lillian
Ong, Yui Big
Ono, Helen
Onofrio, Edna
Opunui, Charles K.
Ortega, Josephine
Ota, Chiyoho
Ota, Iris
Ota, Mike
Otoi, Robert

Pacheco, Herb
Palmese, Emma
Papson, Norman
Paradise, Robert J.
Paris, George
Paris, Jonni
Park, Derek
Patrick, Patricia
Patti, Joan
Paul, Renee
Paul, Victor
Pedroza, Loretta
Pedroza, Robert A.
Pendleton, Charles
Perce, Fred
Perrin, Chip
Perrin, Jack
Petersen, Elsa
Peterson, Harold
Petris, Paula
Pherrin, Virginia
Pineira, Sylvia
Pixley, Melvin
Ploski, Joseph
Poindexter, Byron
Pollack, Anita
Polo, Robert
Porcett, Lucille
Porta, James
Portney, Charlotte
Portugal, Alice
Portugal, Jose
Pourchot, Ray L.
Powers, Warren
Pozzo, Edward M.
Prado, Damita
Pulford, Donald
Punay, Rita
Pyne, Terry

Quan, Henry
Quan, Thomas Y.
Quan, Tung Him
Quen, Wong Chuck
Quesada, Rod
Quigley, Art
Quijada, John
Quon, Alvin
Quon, Duey
Quon, Wallace Moon

Ragone, Concettina
Raisch, William
Ram, Shine
Randall, Tony
Randolph, Dianne
Rapport, Fred

Ravel, Beverly
Ravel, Dianne
Ravenscroft, M.
Ray, Sammy
Raymaster, Leslie
Raymond, Anthony
Raymond, Ford
Reed, Kathryn
Reeves, Robert
Rego, Roland
Reid, Leina Ala
Reid, Max
Rekwart, Waclaw
Remington, Peggy
Revelala, Fred
Reynolds, Fess
Riccardi, Ricky
Rice, John
Richardson, David
Richmond, Leo C.
Ridgeway, Suzanne
Rizzuti, Don
Roberts, Dwight F.
Robinson, Robert
Rochelle, Edwin
Rochin, Aaron
Rochin, Celia
Rochin, Paul
Rode, Walter
Rodriquez, Armando
Rogers, Lloyd
Rojas, Julia
Rome, Betty
Romero, Florita
Rooney, Kathleen
Roosevelt, Buddy
Rose, Bert
Rose, Milt
Ross, George, Jr.
Ross, Joe
Ross, Marion
Roud, Andrew
Rousanville, John
Roux, Antonio
Roy, John
Rubino, Joseph
Rumboa, Sylvester
Rundell, Barbara
Russ, Pola
Russell, George
Russell, Jamie
Russo, Johnnie
Ryan, Dick

Sablon, Loulette
Sack, Tulip Gee
Sadato, Yoshitaro
Sadd, Joe
Saenz, Jose
St. Angeleo, Robert
Saito, John
Sakai, Clifford
Sakato, Henry
Salsbury, James
Sam, Lew
Samova, Tanya
Sanchez, Raymond
Sands, Danny
Santell, George
Santoro, Jack
Sardo, Cosmo
Saruwatari, Noriko
Sato, Edna
Savant, Dean
Savitsky, Gen Sam
Sayre, Jeffrey
Scarpa, Edward
Schaffer, Rube
Scheiwiller, Fred
Scheue, Maria
Schiro, Nancy
Schneider, Joseph Leopold
Scholtman, John
Schoon, Kathleen
Schottland, Millie
Schumacher, Phillip
Schwartz, Harry
Scobie, James
Scott, James Robert
Seal, Peter
Searless, Eddie
Sease, Robert E.
Seaton, Scott
Seba, Duke
Sell, Bernard
Selwyn, James
Semple, Jack
Sesaki, George

Seto, Ya Mee Tuk
Shack, Sammy
Shafer, Earl
Sharon, Dee
Sharp, Clint
She, Lee Tom
Shee, Yee
Sheehan, Bobbie
Sheets, Edith P.
Sheffield, A.
Shelley, Jordan
Sherry, Ariel
Shibata, Amy
Shigezani, Min
Shin, Jack
Shirano, Kumakichi
Siauss, Renato
Siegel, Arthur
Silva, Irene K.
Sing, Chen
Singh, Basanta
Singh, Bhogwan
Singh, R. Lal
Sinka, Bonnie
Sketchley, Leslie
Skluth, Roy
Slay, Charles
Smaney, June
Smaney, Mabel
Smile, Ted
Smith, Albert
Smith, J. Lewis
Smith, Julian
Smith, Michael
Smith, Valerie
Smith, Winona
Snyder, Beverly
Snyder, Don
Snow, Leonard Van
Sohi, Channon
Solari, Ray
Soldani, Charles
Soldi, Stephen
Somova, Tanya
Sonami, Laciba
Song, Mary
Song, Owen Kyoon
Sonkur, Kaluk
Soo Hoo, Eileen
Soo Hoo, Helen
Soo Hoo, Howard
Soo Hoo, Ilene
Soo Hoo, Lester
Soo Hoo, Walter
Soo Hoo, Wo She
Sotomayor, Littlie
Sottile, Annette
Spealman, Colleen
Spence, Edwana
Spencer, Jimmy
Spiker, Ray
Spitz, Fred
Stack, John
Staiger, Scherry
Stamps, Larry
Stanbridge, Ed
Stanley, John
Steckler, Murray
Stein, Anna
Steinberg, Phil
Stephenson, Miles
Stetson, Rita
Stevans, Norman
Stevens, Bert
Stewart, Joy
Stone, Keahi
Stoney, Jack
Stowell, Bruce
Strader, Martin
Strangis, Jane
Strong, Robert
Sui, Kam Wong
Sui, Lianne
Sui, Lily
Suiter, Bill
Sumoze, Mits
Sun, Joseph R.
Sung, Jew
Sung, Richard
Sutherland, Mitzi
Tahir, Mahmed
Tai, Wong
Takaki, Arnold
Tamura, Fumi
Tanino, Tak
Tannahill, Everett
Tarshis, Ruth
Tashireo, Tyra

Tashiro, Tatsu
Taylor, Blanche
Taylor, Maxine
Taylor, Tim
Tellegen, Michael
Teneyck, Lillian
Terril, Terry
Terry, Barbara
Testa, Theresa
Thomas, Delmar
Thomas, Loretta
Thorne, Richard
Thorpe, Ken
Tijero, Julio
Togawa, Kimi
Tom, Allen
Tom, Chon Lem
Tom, C. Y.
Tom, Herb
Tom, Ronald
Tomita, Masu
Tomita, Miyako
Tonkel, Alfred H.
Topetchy, Byron
Tornek, Jack
Tovey, Arthur
Toy, Lee Kay
Trad, Bebe
Truppi, Danny
Tuitama, Kuka
Turbay, Mary
Turner, Blaine

Uchiyamada, Barbara
Udall, Laura
Ugarte, Jr.
Underwood, Evelyn
Ung, Christine
Ung, Fay
Ung, Judy
Urchel, Tony

Valdez, Manuel
Valentine, June
Valerio, Albano
Valetti, Lisle
Van, Charles
Van Dyke, Shirley
Van Horn, James
Varela, Gloria B.
Vasquez, Luz
Veto, Ronald
Vincent, Sailor B.

Yahuhara, Bill
Yamaguchi, Mickey
Yamaka, Harriet
Yarnell, Sally
Yashuhara, Bill
Yashuhara, Phil
Yani, Bob
Ybarra, Conha
Ybarra, Manuel
Ybarra, Roque
Yee, Helen
Yee, Shion Sim
Yee, Shuy Ching
Yim, Archie
Yip, Anna
Yip, Yee Oak
Yokata, William
Yomanchi, Peggy
Yongawa, Yas
Yoshimara, Roy
Yoshimura, Harold
Yoshizaki, Lily
Yoshizaki, Min
Young, Gracie
Young, Mary Lou
Young, May

Zambrano, Ernesto
Zane, Margaret
Zeidman, Allen
Zeithen, Esther
Zuniga, John

ADMINISTRATIVE STAFF

Publicity
UNITED STATES
Bill Doll
Lou Smith
Ernest Anderson
Chuck Cochard
Jack Egan
Seymour Krawitz
Al Sharper
Tom Wood

SPAIN
Juan Luis Calleja

Secretarial
Richard Hanley, *executive secretary, California*
Midori Tsuji, *executive secretary, New York*
Edythe Baird
Mayme Bell
Gladys Benito
Louise Costa
Jack Frost
Margaret Kelly
Liberty Koloniar
Doris Kruse
Renee Laven
Margaret Marsh
Patricia O'Neil
Blanche Pinkussohn
Jordan Ramin
Carol Robertson
Virginia Rowe
Flora Dee Sampson
Adelaide Schneider
Marguerite Smith
Lillian Stewart
Helen Tomlinson
Matilda Wiebel
Patricia Woodward

Accounting
UNITED STATES
Samuel Wien
Gerry Broderick
Sophia Brown
Louis Bernstein
Mazzios Damon
Charles Heiss
Harriet Iskowitz
Ethel King
Albert Kraus
Harold Lindemann
Edna Maguire
William Quinn
John Wooster
LONDON
Irene Jay
Myra Mitford
PARIS
M. Aubart
M. Lavigne
SPAIN
José Boqueron
Felix Fadrique

TECHNICAL STAFF

Art Direction and Sets
UNITED STATES
James Sullivan
Allan Abbott
Eugene Angel
Lois Green Cohen
Lucius O. Croxton
Leroy Deane
George Fowler
Fred Harpman
Ladd Hoffman
Leslie Marzoff
Alexander Mayer
Masaji B. Murai
Steven Pridgeon
Alfred Sheppard
Frank Smith
Marilyn Sotto
Tyrus Wong
LONDON
Ken Adams
Peter Dukelow
Thomas Erley
Joe Hurley
Olga Lehmann
Marjory Whittington
Gilbert Wood
SPAIN
Julio Molina
Juan Albert Soler

Asiatic Unit
PERMANENT STAFF
Kevin McClory, *director*
Thomas Erley, *properties*
Skeets Kelly, *cameraman*
Edward Williams, *technical consultant*

JAPAN
Robert Nakai,
  production manager
Harry Mimura,
  camera operator
A. Matsumoto,
  camera operator
Yanagawa,
  camera operator
J. Karamoto,
  assistant director
C. Watanabe, *stills*
F. James,
  assistant director
Yamada, *make-up*
Shimizu, *wardrobe*
Kazuo Ito, *carpenter*
Sakae Kawakami,
  carpenter
Hashiyama, *electrician*
Odawara Shoten,
  electrician

HONG KONG
Li Chou
Henry Woo
SIAM
Tobi Sac
PAKISTAN
Jobakan Jerry
Karim

Casting
William White
Frank Leyva
Ann Teague

Choreography and Native Dances
Paul Godkin,
  Choreographer
Dancers:
Marie Ardell
Douglas Burnham
Manuela De Herey
Lola De Ronda
Gloria Dewerd
Dolores Ellsworth
John Ferguson
Paul Haakon
Gitanillo Heredia
Gretchen Houser
Leona Irwin
Antonio Jimenez
Joan Kelly
Virginia Lee
John C. Lewis
Charles Lunard
William Lundy
Demita Prado
Anita Ramos
Paul Rees
Joe Rudan
Arthur Sedinger
Pepita Sevilla
Robert Street
Muriel Weldon

Costume Design
UNITED STATES
Miles White
LONDON
Anna Duse
PARIS
M. Cottin
Mme. Rey

Direction
Michael Anderson,
  director
Kevin O'Donovan McClory,
  *director, Asiatic unit and
  Paris sequence*
Sidney Smith, *director,
  documentary unit*
First Assistant Directors:
Ivan Volkman, *Hollywood
  and Durango, Colorado*
Lew Borzage,
  Lawton, Oklahoma
Dennis Bertera, *Spain,
  London and Paris*
Farley James, *Japan*
Second Assistant Directors:
Jack Boland
Joseph C. Boyle

John Chulay
Elmer Decker
Paul Feiner
George Loper
Frank Losee
Buddy Messenger
Michael G. Messenger
Wilbur Mosier
William O'Donnell
L. J. Selznick
Ivan G. Thomas
Arthur R. Thompson

Alfonso Acebal, *Spain*
Cheung, *Hong Kong*
Charles Hammond,
  London and Paris
Jack Karamoto, *Japan*
Isidore Martinez-Ferry,
  Spain

Gino A. Marotta,
  third assistant, London

*Teachers of Children
Appearing in Picture*
Lucie Besag
Mary Dewitt
Marcia Levin
Leon G. Lyons
Georgia Marsh
Ruth Overman
Felippa G. Rock
Ruth Victor

Documentary
Sid Smith, *director*
Asa Clark, *cutter*
John Chulay,
  second assistant director
Wallace Chewning,
  cameraman

Editorial
Paul Weatherwax
Ted Bellinger
Howard Epstein
Donald Tomlinson

Fred Beard, *projectionist*

Electrical
Don C. Stott
Leland Armstrong
William Draper
Albert Gilbert
John D. Glover
Jack Griffith
Norman Lindley
Frank Milliken
John O'Malley
Glenn Pennington
Jess Salais
John Vaiana
Durango, Colorado
Merle Boardman
Harold G. Coulson
Francis E. Grumpp
Thomas B. Lloyd

Floral and Arboreal Decoration
Harold G. Becker
Bruce Bell
Nicholas Carey
William Crider
Richard Huhn
Arthur Lang
Myron C. Peterson
Abe Siegel
William Steck
Robert Villegas
Lou Honig, *Contractor*

Hair Styling
UNITED STATES
Edith Keon

Peggy Adams
Jane Aldrich
Cherie Banks
Sally Berkeley
Yvette Bernier
Lillian Burkhart
Eleanor Cole
Madine Danks
Elizabeth Detter

Katharina Detter
Lily Dirigo
Doris Durkus
Emmy Eckhardt
Ray Forman
Wava Green
Carla M. Hadley
Doris Haines
Dotha Hippe
Hazel Keithley
Ann E. Kirk
Hazel Kraft
Fritzy La Bar
Lillian Lashin
Annabell Levy (ch)
Maudlee MacDougall
Peggy McDonald
Wenda McKee
Mildred Margulies
Louise Miehle
Eve Newing
Lily Rader
Francesca Raffa
Gladys Rasmussen
Gertrude Reade
Merle Reeves
Leonora Sabine
Ruth Sandifer
Katherine Shea
Lillian Shore
Fae M. Smith
Josephine Sweeney
Hazel R. Thompson
Peg Thomson
Marion Vaugh
LONDON
Bette Lee
PARIS
M. Archambault
SPAIN
Puyol-Suarez

Logistics
UNITED STATES
Pilots
Paul Mantz
Merle Edgerton
Stanley Reaver

Drivers
Robert Jamieson
George F. Andrews
Leroy A. Beach
Don Bell
William S. Bethea
John Cooley
Frank Coon
Russell Coon
Ike Danning
William Ford
Albert Frederickson
Wilbur Freese
Emil Garner
Orville Hebert
Irving Hedeen
Cecil Higgins
William Hoxie
R. W. Hutchinson
Horace Irwin
John F. Jackson
John Jay Jones
Edwin Kemp
Wilkie Kleinpell
Norman Knighton
John A. O'Hare
Peter Pitassi
Nick Potskoff
Allee G. Reed
Ernest A. Reed
Edward Ritchie
Paul Romero
Hal H. Smith
George Spahn, Jr.
William Trow
James R. White
UNITED STATES
Drivers—Durango, Colorado
Ernest F. Austin
R. A. Beirley
Beryl D. Benham
Edward Douglas Brown
John D. Brown
Charles Robert Carter
William H. Craig
Pat L. Cugnini
Melvin V. Flack
Bennie Legill
Carl H. Longstrom

William Loftus
Henry C. Ludwig
Charles Harry Meador
Chester W. Meador
Samuel H. Miller
James A. Norton
Shirley B. Palmer
William A. Pryor
Robert Bruce Robertson
Edgar A. Rowe
Fred M. Rudy
Bennet B. St. John
Harold A. Schaaf
SPAIN
José Carmona

Make-Up
UNITED STATES
Gustaf Norin
Bunny Armstrong
Carl Axzelle
George T. Bau
Charles F. Blackman
Willard Buell
E. J. Butterworth, Jr.
Larry Butterworth
Jack Byron
E. Thomas Case, Jr.
Jack Casey
Jean Casey
John Chambers
Steven Clensos
Robert Cowan
Robert Dawn
Armand Delmar
Violette De Noyer
Russel Drake
Willon Fields
Charles Gemora
George G. Gray
H. Dan Greeneway
Lee Greeneway
Burris Grimwood
Joseph Hadley
Richard Hamilton
Robert Hickman
Louis Hippe
Gordon Hubbard
John A. D. Johnson
Newton J. Jones
A. C. Karnagel
Claire Kaufman
Grant Keats
Benjamin Lane
Ted Larsen
Frank La Rue
Charles Lauder
Harold Lierly
Robert Littlefield
Raymond Lopez
Stanley McKay
Otis Malcolm
Paul Malcolm
Harry Maret
Bob Mark
Terry Miles
Thomas P. Miller, Jr.
Imogene Mollner
Bill Morley
Garret W. Morris
Dick Narr
William Oakley
Jack Obringer
Stanley Orr
E. W. Overlander
Ernie Park
Sidney Perell
Louis Phillipi
Fred Phillips
H. W. Phillips
Webster C. Phillips
Sam Polo
Mark Reedall
Lynn Reynolds
Ray Romero
Harry Ross
Carl A. Russell
Philip Scheer
Walter Schenck
Don Schoenfeld
Charles Schram
Erroll K. Silvera
Gloria Skarstedt
Jack M. Smith
Allan Snyder
Leland Stanfield
Paul Stanhope, Jr.
John A. Stone
Daniel Striepke

John F. Sweeney
Claude M. Thompson
William P. Turner
Thomas Tuttle
Nicholas Vehr
Fred T. Walker
John Wallace
Fred Williams
Joe Williams
Alice Wills
Edith Wilson
William D. Wood
E. Jean Young
Edward Zimmer

LONDON
John O'Gorman
Tom Smith
PARIS
Mme. Archambault
Mme. Barsky
M. Bordenave
M. Bouban
M. Bouban
M. de Fast
Mme. Gasperina
M. Gauthier
Mlle. Gilet
M. Gleboff
M. Klein
Mme. Knapp
Mme. Lemoigne
Mme. Milhau
M. Neant
M. Neant
Mme. Ouvrard
M. Quentin
M. Pallazolo
M. Svoboda
Mme. Trieste
SPAIN
Alonso
JAPAN
Yamada (*also on Asiatic Unit*)

Music
Victor Young
Jay Blackton
Leo Abbey
Benny Ahuna
Nestor Amaral
Albert C. Anderson
Norman Bennett
Russell Blough
Dan Borzage
Stanley W. Cha
Irwin Charles
Jack Costanzo
Eugene David
Johnnie David
Charles De Pietro
Robert Dival
Satya Pal Dosaj
George Drexler
Calvin Earl
Joseph Eger
James Fernandez
Pete Ferrara
Aluisio Ferreira
Don Ferris
Bert Gassman
Ronald Gay
Al Gayle
Robert D. Gilbert
Joseph Glasser
Bhupesh C. Guha
Arnold Haber
Bernard Haber
Robert Helfer
Joe Heredia
Wally Hersom
Milton Holland
Frank Iseri
Matsukichi Kamo
Dave Kapua
Thomas Karasawa
Allan Kila
Charles Knox
Frank Konyi
Allen Kramer
Eddie La Freniere
Vale Leitner
Meyer J. Leslie
Al Linden
Carroll K. Londoner
Mitchell Lurie
J. S. MacDuff
Sheldon Manne
Henry Maurey

Al Michaelian
Allia T. Miller
Thomas Mills
Leslie Moe
Pasupati Mukerjee
Joe Oliveira
Wendell Olsen
Henry Onishi
John H. Onishi
Brojeswar Pakrasi
Lee Perrin
Harley Pitts
Neely Plumb
Ernest Pometti
Charles Prieste
Sam H. Rice
Ramon Rivera
Robert Roberti
Sylvia Ruderman
Douglas Sakamoto
Donald Shaw
Takeshi Shindo
August Sill
Hal Silverstone
Donald G. Smith
Lew Snowden
Paul Sprosty
Al Starr
Elwood Strawsbury
Robert Stevens
Gordon Steventon
James Talbert
Joseph Valenti
William Vandenburg
J. V. Villarino
Tommy Walker
Stanley West
Gordon Willey
Earl Williams
Emanuel Woen
Harold Woodland
Marvin Wright
Joseph Zito

Singers
Burton Dole
Zarubi Elmassian
Bill Lee
Ray Linn
Betty Mulliner
Robert Nadell
Ernest Newton
Loulie J. Norman
Thurl Ravenscroft
Virginia Rees
William Reeve
Charles Schroeder
Marie G. Vernon
Tudor Williams

Photography
UNITED STATES
Lionel Lindon
William N. Williams, *first*
cameraman for animation
Landon Arnett
Alfred Baalas
Donald H. Birnkrant
Haskell Boggs
Emilio Calori
Ellis Carter
Edward Chaffin
Alfred Cline
Walter Craig
James Daly
Jock Feindel
James Grout
Harold Harmon
S. J. Hoffberg
Roy Ivey
Richard Kline
A. Lindsley Lane
George Le Picard, Sr.
Cliff MacDonald
F. Mautino
Harry Parsons
Otto Pierce
William Rankin
Maynard B. Rugg
Lester Shorr
George Smart
William Snyder
Charles Straumer
Charles Termini
John D. Weiler
Jock Wendall

LONDON
Neil Binney
Bill Bonner

R. Bryce
Kenneth Clark
Kevin Kavanagh
Graham Kelly
Stan Sayer
E. H. Williams
PARIS
M. Bontemps
M. Clunie
M. Domage
M. Letouzey
Mlle. Massey
SPAIN
Manuel Berenguer
Luis Macasoli
JAPAN
(also listed on Asiatic Unit)
A. Matsumoto
Harry Mimura
Yanagawa

Production
UNITED STATES
Frank Fox, *unit manager*
Don Bruno, *set construction*
  and operation co-ordinator
Electricians
Don C. Stott
Leland Armstrong
William Draper
Albert Gilbert
John D. Glover
Jack Griffith
Norman Lindley
Frank Milliken
John O'Malley
Glenn Pennington
Jess Salais
John Vaiana
Durango, Colorado
Merle Boardman
Harold G. Coulson
Francis E. Grumpp
Thomas B. Lloyd
Painters
W. R. Moore
Alex Sinel
Alfred Stroup
Grips
John Akers
Alvin R. Cannon
Louis Kusley
Martin Kusley
Bruce Long
George Rader
Karl Reed
Saul Selznick
Marvin Wilson
Laborers
Owen Davies
Frank Grendetta
Richard A. Rabis
Victor Ramos
Dick Stoll
LONDON
Cecil Ford
Cecil Foster Kemp
PARIS
M. Bar
M. Boisserand
M. Bokanowski
M. de Masure
M. Denis
M. Germain
M. Lahet
M. Rey
M. Rosen
M. Sursin
M. Viriot
SPAIN
Alfonso Acebal
Luis Berraquero
Alfredo Ruescas
Juanito Solorzano
JAPAN
Robert Nakai

Properties
UNITED STATES
Anthony Lombardo
Jack Gorton
John Graffeo
Jack Hallett

Ralph Harris
Willard Hartman
George MacQuarrie
Earl McKee
Paul Melnick
PARIS
M. Doublet
M. Dumousseau
SPAIN
Luna
Angel Sevillano

Research and
Technical Advisors
Research
UNITED STATES
Ann Perls
LONDON
Charles Beard
A. Appleson
Maude Spector
Technical Advisors
Eddie Box
Ernest Greenwalt
Koichi Kawana
George Kishketon
Edgar Monetathchi
Francis Shields
Reginald Lal Singh
Tyrus Wong
PARIS
Mme. Lourie

Set Decoration
UNITED STATES
Ross Dowd
Les Hallett
James A. Lee
George McCrearie
Edward Parker
Allan Price
Barnard Schoefelt
Harold Worthington
PARIS
M. Hinkis
M. Paris
M. Thibault
Mme. Thibault

Sound
UNITED STATES
Joseph Kane
G. R. Danner
William Griffith
Guy Ingersoll
Clarence P. Kelley
John Rixley
Marvin Stoltz
Kenneth Wesson
LONDON
T. R. Cotter
F. Hales
G. Saunders

Special Effects
UNITED STATES
Lee Zavitz
W. Roy Bolton
Robert N. Bonning
John Christensen
Jack Faggard
Joseph Goss
C. B. Handley
Daniel Hays
Louis Hopper
Boat Crew
R. N. Acquistapace
Norman Breedlove
R. S. Cline
Gustav Eriksson
George Harris
Daniel W. Lee
Wiley Medearis
Fred Mitchke
Kenneth Nelson
Merle C. Newby
Leon H. Paquet
Kenneth Sneed
R. C. Stangler
Jesse J. Stone
Robert A. Tait
Jerry Welker
PARIS
Mme. Dunan

JAPAN
Kazuo Ito
Sakae Kawakami

Still Cameramen
UNITED STATES
Don Christie
Jack Albin
Ernest Bachrach
William Cary
Milton Gold
Newton Hopcraft
Clifton L. Kling
Madison Lacy
Talmadge Morrison
Leonard Powers
William E. Thomas
LONDON
Ken Danvers
James Swarbrick

Wardrobe
UNITED STATES
Robert Martien
Hazel Allensworth
Charles Arrico
Eugene Ashman
Norma Brown
Frank Budz
Frank Cardinale
Veda Caroll
Mildred Duncan
Elmer Ellsworth
Ann Fielder
Leona Forman
William Jobe, Jr.
Norman Martien
G. L. Merrill, Jr.
Lillian Orr
Marie Osborn
Theodore Parvin
Bernice Pontrelli
Carl Steppling
Thelma Strahm
Sophia Stutz
James W. Wallace
LONDON
Betty Adamson
Monty Berman
Harry Jourdan
Janet Lesley
PARIS
Mme. Alaphilippe
Mme. Banguarel
Mme. Baudot
M. Capel
M. Chivalie
Mme. Chivalie
M. Gasnier
M. Manza
Mme. Manza
M. Radenane
Mme. Revillard
Mme. Sekeder
M. Vittonatto
SPAIN
José Baquera
Cornejo
Seamstresses:
Justine Cavaliere
Anita Duran
Tailor:
William Guzik

Wrangling
(Animal Handling)
Kenneth Lee
Sam Ashton
David Baker
Richard Brehm
James Campbell
Minyard Caudill
Harley Chambers
Ray Chandler
Edward W. Clark
Delmer Combs
Sam Cook
Howard Cramer
Robert F. Dick
Edward Duarte
Jean W. Eaton
Leslie Elder
Walter D. Elliott
George Emerson
Homer Farra

Jeff Flores
Milton Galbraith
Eugene Goebel
L. C. Goss
Clinton C. Hall
Marceline J. Herrara
Tony Gilbert Herrera
William Hines
Wayne Hobson
William L. Hostetter
William Howe
Harry Hupp
Kenneth L. Jenkins
Ben Johnson
A. W. Kennard
Alvin Kimsey
Frank Klump
William Koehler
Adam Krackenberger
Frank D. Lane
Richard A. Lee
Kester Lipscomb
Joe Lomax
John McDonald
William McNally
Charles McQuary
Burt Mattox
George Myers
Walter Noble
Fox O'Callahan
Albert Parker
Frank Potts
Russell Ray
Fess Reynolds
Alvin T. Reed
Henry Herbert Reed
A. F. Reinhardt
D. B. Richardson
D. B. Richardson, Jr.
Lee Roberson
Claude L. Robinson
Alfred Roelker
Wallace C. Ross
Frank R. Sanders
Carl Scarsdale
Oscar Schaaf
Jack Shannon
Elmo Slade
Jack E. Smith
Drew Stanfield
Henry Tyndall
Norman Walke
Richard Webb
Mike Wiciniski
Leonard Douglas Winbourn
Robert Yankie

OTHER PERSONNEL
Boat Crew on the
  Henrietta
Robert E. Lee, Captain
Everett D. Klaumann,
  First mate
Edward Silva,
  Ship's engineer
Police Attachés
CALIFORNIA
Herb Felsen
SPAIN
Paulino Domingo
First Aid
FRANCE
Larry Bump
Sidney Kruger
John Leber
Radio Operator
Willard Starr
S.P.C.A. Representative
Jimmy Jack
Script Supervision
Betty Levin
Script Clerks
UNITED STATES
John Franco
LONDON
Kay Rawlings
PARIS
Mme. Lecouffe
Maid in Durango
Lena Henderson
Watchman in Durango
Joe C. Valdez

"Michael Todd's show makes this a better world"

Mark Barron, Associated Press

"Delightful Fun and an Absolute Triumph of Imagination, Gaiety and Showmanship."

RICHARD WATTS, JR.